Book

Dag Heward-Mills

Order your copy online today at
www.daghewardmills.org

Facebook: Dag Heward-Mills
Twitter: EvangelistDag

How to Pray

DAG HEWARD-MILLS

Parchment House

First published 2013 by Parchment House
3rd Printing 2014

Find out more about Dag Heward-Mills at:

Healing Jesus Campaign
Write to: evangelist@daghewardmills.org
Website: www.daghewardmills.org
Facebook: Dag Heward-Mills
Twitter: @EvangelistDag

ISBN : 978-9988-8550-5-5

Contents

Chapter 1

If You Are Too Busy to Pray Then You Are Too Busy

Now when Daniel knew that the writing was signed, he went into his house; and his windows being open in his chamber toward Jerusalem, he kneeled upon his knees three times a day, and prayed, and gave thanks before his God, as he did aforetime.

Daniel 6:10

Anyone who is too busy to pray is too busy. No matter who you are, you cannot allow yourself to become too busy to pray. You will notice from the Scripture above that Daniel prayed three times a day. An important phrase used in this verse is "as he did aforetime". That means that Daniel had been praying these prayers on a regular basis. Daniel was not just praying because he was in trouble; he had a habit of praying.

Many times when people become prosperous they stop going for prayer meetings and eventually backslide. Not so with Daniel! He was the Prime Minister of his country, second in authority only to the king. He was a successful man who had risen from slavery to the high office of Prime Minister. He was one of the most respected and feared men in the nation. He was a major politician of the day. He was a civil servant. Yet, he prayed three times a day, *every day*!

What were the principles that guided Daniel to have such an unusual and consistent prayer time? Here they are, read them and let them become *your* principles. You too can have the success that Daniel had. I want you to read through, study and analyze the following principles that I believe guided Daniel in his life.

Principle No. 1: Prayer Is Very Important

Someone once said that it is more important to know how to pray than to have a degree from the university. There are many things that are important in this life. A good education is important. Money is important. A good marriage is important. But, *a good prayer life is most important!*

Let this enter your spirit — *in all your getting, get prayer!* In all your activities, make room for prayer!

Principle No. 2: No One Is Ever Too Busy, Too Blessed or Too Successful to Pray

You may have a busy life style and you may be a very important person; however, I do not think that you are busier than Daniel was. Daniel was a Prime Minister, a leader in the nation. Many people think that Heads of State and Ministers of government have a relaxed and enjoyable life, flying all over the world. That is not true! I am the head of a large organization myself, and I know that people in high positions do not have an easy life. The higher you go, the greater the responsibility you have.

There is so much hard work involved in staying on the cutting edge of life and ministry. Did you know that successful executives like Daniel are so stressed out that they are prone to diseases like stomach ulcers and heart attacks? These conditions are more common with very busy people because of the hard work that they do.

Daniel was one such person. He was a Prime Minister, yet he felt that he was not too busy to pray three times a day. **If you think you are too busy to pray, then you are deceiving yourself.** If you do not pray, it is because you do not want to pray. It is because you do not think that prayer is important now! Daniel was successful, yet he prayed. Why was he able to pray three times a day?

People have grown out of poverty and into prosperity. When they were poor, they had a lot of time to attend prayer meetings. But when they became blessed, they felt everything was all right. No! Everything is not all right! Your prosperity is not the signal to stop praying.

Principle No. 3: Prayer is the Source of Our Power and Protection

You must realize that it is prayer which releases the power of God on our behalf. Jesus knew the power of prayer. That is why he spent long hours in prayer. Maybe you are a successful businessman, and you do not think that you need any of this spiritual "stuff". Perhaps you are a politician and you think your protection must come from fetish or occult powers.

Let me tell you right now, there is power in prayer. We do not need any other power when we have the power of prayer. There is protection for us when we pray. The last part of the armour of God is prayer (Ephesians 6:18). In other words, prayer is an important part of your spiritual defence.

Many people become afraid when they prosper. Job was filled with fear when he prospered. Eventually he said, "What I feared greatly has happened to me". Such people feel that somebody may use supernatural powers to try to kill them. You have nothing to fear when you are a prayerful person like Daniel. Many people wanted to kill Daniel. These people did not just think about killing Daniel, they actually tried to eliminate him. Through the power of prayer, Daniel was protected from the lions.

I see all the lions in your life scattering away in fear! I see your prayer power rising! I see you going forward because of a new-found prayer life!

...that Jesus also being baptized, and praying, the heaven was opened,

Luke 3:21

3

I see the heavens opening over your life! Never forget this! The heavens opened when Jesus prayed. Both physical and spiritual blessings rain upon you when you are a prayerful person.

Principle No. 4: Prayer Is Important in Acquiring and Sustaining the Blessings of God

Do you have anything that you are proud of? Have you achieved anything in this life? Let me tell you that it is by the grace of God. By the power of prayer, you will achieve even greater things. It is by prayer that you will sustain what God has placed in your hands.

There are people who have received thousands of dollars as gifts. Today, that money has disappeared into thin air. God may give you something but it also takes His grace to sustain that blessing. Are you the pastor of a great ministry? Let me tell you, it takes prayer to sustain you in the ministry. Why do you think Jesus kept running away to pray?

There is a law of degeneration at work in the world. Everything is decaying. Your business is decaying. Your church is decaying. Your very life is decaying. It takes the power of God, through prayer, to preserve everything that God has given to you.

Principle No. 5: For Prayer to Be Effective It Must Be Habitual

A man called Dostoyevsky said, "The second half of a man's life is made up of the habits he acquired in the first half."

Pascal said, "The strength of a man's virtues is made up of his habitual acts."

If you are going to be a great person in this life, you need to have good habits. An action becomes a habit when it is repeated many times; sometimes consciously, other times unconsciously. It becomes your custom!

4

Habits can be either good or bad. Remember that good habits are repeated as easily as bad habits. A good habit will lead to consistent breakthroughs even without you intending it to. Bad habits will also lead to consistent failure.

If you decide to develop a habit of prayer, you are developing a habit for success. Jesus went to church on the Sabbath because it was his habit. The Bible tells us that Jesus had customs or habits.

...as his custom [habit] was, he went into the synagogue on the sabbath day...

Luke 4:16

Daniel had a custom of praying three times a day.

...he [Daniel] kneeled upon his knees three times a day, and prayed...

Daniel 6:10

Life in the secular world is not designed to include a prayer time. Work starts early in the morning and continues late into the night. Weeks may pass before you even think of prayer. For many people, it is only an impossible situation that reminds them of the need for prayer. Dear friend, it is important for you to include prayer in your life.

God is not a spare tyre! A spare tyre is something that is never used except in emergencies. God is no fool. Whatsoever a man sows, he will reap. If you have time for God on a regular basis, He will have time to bless you on a regular basis. Only the mercy of God makes Him listen to some of our prayers.

Develop your prayer life until it happens spontaneously. Develop your prayer life until you pray habitually without even thinking of what you are doing.

I Made Time to Pray

When I was a medical student, I was very busy with my coursework. There was no time to pray at all. But because I had

5

made prayer a part of my Christian life, there was no way I could do without it! I had to somehow include it in my schedule. I decided to pray late at night. I was usually so sleepy that I had to walk about just to stay awake. Prayer was so important to me that I could not leave it out of my life.

One night, as I headed for my room after one of such prayer times, I actually fell asleep whilst walking! It was only when I walked into the Spanish Department building of the university that I woke up from my sleep! I believe that God saw my earnest desire to keep praying in spite of an impossible medical school schedule.

Principle No. 6: Prayer Must Continue Both in Troubled Times and in Times of Peace

Why do we wait for trouble before we pray? Would you take someone as a serious friend if he only called you when he was in serious trouble? In times of peace, he had no time for you. God is looking for someone who will fellowship with Him in both good and bad times.

The more I preach, the better I become at preaching. The more you pray, the better you will become at prayer. In times of crises, you will find yourself rising up to the occasion and delivering powerful prayers that bring results.

Principle No. 7: Every Nation Needs Lots of Prayer and Prayerful Leaders

There is no doubt that the world is ruled by wicked spirits in high places. The earth is filled with people who are at war with each other. Famine, war, epidemics and disasters abound! You just have to keep your eyes on the international news and you will hear about another major disaster.

Dictators of all kinds abound in many nations. Like snakes, which shed their skin, many dictators of yesteryear have a new "democratic look".

Many national leaders are actually under the influence of evil spirits, and that makes them do the things they do. They cling to power instead of honourably allowing others to have a chance at leadership. Like vampires, they drink the blood of the nation's wealth and stack it away in secret places.

Political leaders like Hitler lead entire nations into initial prosperity, and then eventual destruction. I always remember how things changed in South Africa after President De Klerk replaced President Botha. A new leader led to the release of Nelson Mandela and the end of apartheid. It is important for us to pray for these leaders so that our nation will prosper. The right person at the helm of affairs will make a lot of difference to our nation. I believe that the presence of a prayerful person like Daniel made a lot of difference to that nation.

Principle No. 8: It is Important to Pray for Long Periods of Time

Years ago, the only prayers I knew about were those that the priests read out to us in church. The longest I could pray was thirty to forty seconds and that was when I recited the Lord's Prayer. There were three prayers I knew how to pray: The Lord's Prayer, Hail Mary and a Prayer to the Angel of God! However, as I grew in the Lord I learnt how to pray for myself. I can now pray for several hours at a time.

I always remember the first time I prayed for three hours. I was a student in Achimota School (Prince of Wales College). I was in the midst of a crisis and I needed the intervention of the Lord. I can also remember the first time I prayed for seven hours. I was a sixth-former in the same Achimota School. I prayed from 10 a.m. to 5 p.m. I enjoy praying for long hours.

Praying for thirty minutes is almost like no prayer to me. Do not misunderstand me; I am not saying that God does not hear short prayers. I am saying that I have developed the art of praying for long hours like Jesus did. Jesus prayed for three hours in the garden of Gethsemane.

And he went a little further, and fell on his face, and prayed... And he cometh unto the disciples, and findeth them asleep, and saith unto Peter, What, COULD YE NOT WATCH WITH ME ONE HOUR?

He went away again the second time, and prayed... And he came and found them asleep again: for their eyes were heavy. And he left them, and went away again, and prayed the third time, saying the same words.

Matthew 26:39,40,42-44

In this Scripture, Jesus was surprised that the disciples could not pray for one hour.

And he cometh unto the disciples, and findeth them asleep, and saith unto Peter, What, could ye not watch with me one hour?

Matthew 26:40

Jesus prayed all night before he chose His disciples.

And it came to pass in those days, that he went out into a mountain to pray, and continued all night in prayer to God.

And when it was day, he called unto him his disciples: and of them he chose twelve, whom also he named apostles;

Luke 6:12,13

Long prayer may not be an explicit instruction in the Bible, but it is implicit throughout the Word. In later chapters I will teach you what to pray about when you decide to pray for long hours.

Principle No. 9: It is Important to Enter Your Closet for Effective Prayer

Many Christians can only pray when they are in a group. They cannot stay in a room on their own and pray for one hour. That is a great handicap. **There is a difference between praying alone and praying with a group of people.** Both types of prayer are important. If you can pray for three hours on your own then you can pray for six hours with other people. It is easier to pray in a group. Each time, you expand your ability to pray alone, you are expanding your ability to chalk great achievements in prayer.

Principle No. 10: Everyone Must Develop the Ability and the Formulae for Praying Four Times a Day

There are four important times to pray: Morning, afternoon, evening and all-the-time.

Jesus prayed in the morning!

And in the morning, rising up a great while before day, he went out, and departed into a solitary place, and there prayed.

Mark 1:35

What is so important about morning prayer? Prayer in the morning is very good because you meet God before you meet the devil. You meet God before you meet the circumstances of life. God anoints you to overcome every mountain that you will encounter in your life.

Prayer in the afternoon signifies prayer in the midst of activities.

And when he had sent them away, he departed into a mountain to pray.

Mark 6:46

When you pray in the afternoon, it signifies that in the heat of the day and in the thick of the battle, you recognize God as the most important force in your life. God will bless you for afternoon prayer. I see you praying in the afternoon!

You can take a little time off your lunch break and pray. That prayer will do you more good than a plate of rice will!

It is also important to pray in the evenings. When the Bible says "watch and pray", it does not mean keep your eyes open when you pray. What it actually means is, stay awake and pray.

And it came to pass in those days, that he went out into a mountain to pray, and continued all night in prayer to God.

Luke 6:12

There is something about praying in the night that is different from praying during the day. It is a very different experience. I have heard that witches are very active around 2 a.m. in the night. Perhaps when you pray in the night you are tackling the forces of darkness in a different way. After all, they are called the forces of darkness (night).

The fourth important time to pray is "all-the-time".

Pray without ceasing.

1 Thessalonians 5:17

Prayer is intended to be a never-ending stream of communication with your Heavenly Father. He has given us the baptism of the Holy Spirit and the gift of speaking in tongues. I pray all the time. My wife tells me that sometimes I pray in my sleep!

Pray without ceasing.

1 Thessalonians 5:17

You can pray on the bus and on your way to work. You can pray softly to yourself when you are in the office. You can pray when you are in the shower. God is happy when His children are constantly in touch with Him.

I have a friend whose wife calls him on his mobile phone at least seven times a day. I have been in meetings with him when he received not less that four calls from his wife. Nothing important, she was just keeping in touch! I think it is a nice thing. She phones without ceasing!

You can also pray without ceasing! I see you praying in the morning and in the evening! God is changing your life because of your new-found prayer life! Your marriage, business and ministry will never be the same by the time you finish reading this book!

When, like Daniel, you decide to pray for long hours, you will discover that you will need to have a pattern or a formula for prayer. You need something that will guide you in your prayer life. In these next chapters, we will study the formulae for prayer.

Daniel's Principles of Prayer

- Prayer is very important.
- No one is ever too busy, too blessed or too successful to pray.
- Prayer is the source of our power and protection.
- Prayer is important in acquiring and sustaining the blessings of God.
- For prayer to be effective, it must be habitual.
- Prayer must continue both in troubled times and in times of peace.
- Every nation needs lots of prayer and prayerful leaders.
- It is important to pray for long periods of time.
- It is important to enter your closet for effective prayer.
- Everyone must develop the ability and the formulae for praying four times a day.

Chapter 2

Why Prayer is Mysterious

But in the days of the voice of the seventh angel, when he shall begin to sound, THE MYSTERY OF GOD should be finished, as he hath declared to his servants the prophets.

Revelation 10:7

Prayer is mysterious because God is mysterious! God is mysterious and there is nothing we can do about it! If you think you will ever know everything about God then you must think again! God is not a man and we cannot know everything about Him. The Scripture above tells us that God is a mystery. The mystery of God will be finished in the days of the voice of the seventh angel. Until then, we are going to have to navigate our lives through the mysteries of God.

It is precisely because of the mysteries surrounding God that a lot of people do not pray. These mysteries should not keep us from prayer but rather draw us closer in search of answers. So what are the mysteries of prayer?

1. **Mysteriously, it seems that God is limited or restricted to do only what we ask. It seems God will not act unless we pray.**

But God came to Abimelech in a dream by night, and said to him, Behold, *thou art* but a dead man, for the woman which thou hast taken; for she is a man's wife.

But Abimelech had not come near her: and he said, Lord, wilt thou slay also a righteous nation?

Said he not unto me, She is my sister? and she, even she herself said, He is my brother: in the integrity of my heart and innocency of my hands have I done this.

And GOD SAID UNTO HIM IN A DREAM, Yea, I know that thou didst this in the integrity of thy heart; for I also withheld thee from sinning against me: therefore suffered I thee not to touch her.

Now therefore restore the man his wife; for he is a prophet, and HE SHALL PRAY FOR THEE, AND THOU SHALT LIVE: and if thou restore her not, know thou that thou shalt surely die, thou, and all that are thine.

Genesis 20:3-7

All through the Bible, you see God moving when He is asked to move. We even see God asking human beings to ask Him to move. In the famous story of Abimelech and Abraham, Abimelech got into serious trouble for taking Abraham's wife as one of his concubines. God appeared to Abimelech in a vision and asked Abimelech to tell Abraham to pray to Him so that Abimelech would not be cursed.

Even though God was talking to Abimelech directly, He told Abimelech *to tell Abraham to ask Him*. Couldn't God have just resolved the matter since He was discussing it with Abimelech directly?

It seems that God wanted or needed Abraham to ask Him before He did anything!

It seems that God would not do anything unless Abraham asked Him! It seemed that God was limited or restricted to do only what Abraham asked for!

It seemed that God would not act unless Abraham asked for it!

God seems to be limited by our prayer lives. This is truly mysterious. How can the creator of Heaven and earth be limited by my prayers? This spurs me on and encourages me to get into the closet and start praying. If God is limited by my prayers then I must spend a lot of time praying and asking Him for things.

2. Mysteriously, even though God knows everything He still wants us to ask about what He already knows.

Why on earth should we tell God about everything that He already knows?

If I already knew that a bomb had been found at the bottom of the lake, why would I want somebody to spend another thirty minutes telling me about the bomb at the bottom of the lake?

It does not make sense for someone to have to listen to things that he already knows.

But, mysteriously, it seems that even though God knows everything, He still wants you to come to Him and tell Him about what He already knows. Is that not amazing?

Be not ye therefore like unto them: for YOUR FATHER KNOWETH WHAT THINGS YE HAVE NEED OF, BEFORE YE ASK HIM.

Matthew 6:8

We also know that God is a good leader and the best father of us all. Unlike some governments that have to be reminded about their citizens' problems, God does not need to be reminded about our problems. Many governments need to be prompted and reminded by strikes and industrial action. But God does not need such prompting because He remembers and knows everything.

The big question is why does God want to be constantly asked and reminded about things that he knows we need? Doesn't He get bored with these old issues that He knows all about?

But He seems to want us to come again and again and to present to Him things that He already knows. What a mystery!

3.   Mysteriously, God seems to want us to keep asking about the same things even though we have asked Him before.

Pray without ceasing.

1 Thessalonians 5:17

If God did not know about our problems on the first day, He must know our problems and our needs by the third day of our prayer. If He knows all things so well, why does He require us to keep coming back to Him? Can we not just ask once?

Why should we pray without ceasing? Why did Jesus tell us the story of the unjust judge who had to be called on persistently until he acted? Is God like the unjust judge who does not know, does not care and does not remember?

If God has a different character why do we have to keep going back to Him with the same issues? Can't He just answer our prayers after we have made one request?

4.   Mysteriously, it seems that God wants us to keep asking but also finds some prayers repetitious and boring.

So which of the prayers should we keep on praying without ceasing and which ones are repetitious and boring to God? This is also a mystery. It is not easy to solve or answer these questions.

But these mysteries must not keep us away from prayer. We must keep on praying to God and He will answer our prayers. We will become experienced as we walk with Him and we will learn what to say and when to say it.

But when ye pray, use not vain repetitions, as the heathen do: for they think that they shall be heard for their much speaking. Be not ye therefore like unto them: for your Father knoweth what things ye have need of, before ye ask him.

Matthew 6:7-8

5. Mysteriously, it seems that some prayers need to be very long, whilst other prayers can be very short.

Throughout the ministry of Jesus we see this mysterious blend of very short prayers as well as very long prayers. So when should we pray a long prayer and when should we pray a short prayer?

Could it be that it is a time to pray a long prayer and we mistakenly pray short prayers? Could we be making terrible mistakes in the types of prayers we are praying?

Could it be the time for a very short prayer, only for us to irritate God with long repeated petitions?

Jesus' weaving between long and short prayers is one of the mysteries of prayer. Sometimes He prayed for a long time and at other times He prayed for a short time. I don't think we have answers to all these mysteries but we must still persist in prayer.

Notice some of the long and short prayers of Jesus. Interestingly, He prayed short prayers at very critical moments of His ministry. Amazingly, the short prayers brought about some of the most fantastic miracles of all time.

Long Prayers in the Wilderness

Then was Jesus led up of the Spirit into the wilderness to be tempted of the devil. And when he had fasted forty days and forty nights, he was afterward an hungred.

Matthew 4:1-2

Long Prayers at Dawn

And in the morning, rising up A GREAT WHILE BEFORE day, he went out, and departed into a solitary place, AND THERE PRAYED.

Mark 1:35

Long Prayers in the Mountain to Choose the Disciples

And it came to pass in those days, that he went out into a mountain to pray, and continued all night in prayer to God.

And when it was day, he called *unto him* his disciples: and of them he chose twelve, whom also he named apostles;

Luke 6:12-13

Long Prayers in the Garden of Gethsemane

And he cometh unto the disciples, and findeth them asleep, and saith unto Peter, What, COULD YE NOT WATCH WITH ME ONE HOUR?

Watch and pray, that ye enter not into temptation: the spirit indeed is willing, but the flesh is weak.

He went away again the second time, and PRAYED, saying, O my Father, if this cup may not pass away from me, except I drink it, thy will be done.

Matthew 26:40-42

Long Prayers for Unity

These words spake Jesus, and lifted up his eyes to heaven, and said, Father, the hour is come; glorify thy Son, that thy Son also may glorify thee:

John 17:1

Short Prayers to Raise the Dead

Then they took away the stone *from the place* where the dead was laid. And JESUS LIFTED UP HIS EYES, AND SAID, FATHER, I THANK THEE THAT THOU HAST HEARD ME.

And I knew that thou hearest me always: but because of the people which stand by I said it, that they may believe that thou hast sent me.

And WHEN HE THUS HAD SPOKEN, HE CRIED with a loud voice, Lazarus, come forth.

John 11:41-43

Short Prayers for the Sick

And Jesus said unto the centurion, Go thy way; and as thou hast believed, so be it done unto thee. And his servant was healed in the selfsame hour.

Matthew 8:13

Short Prayer for Forgiveness
of the Sins of the World

Then said Jesus, Father, forgive them; for they know not what they do. And they parted his raiment, and cast lots.

Luke 23:34

6. Mysteriously, it seems we can reason with and negotiate with God.

The prophet Isaiah calls on human beings to reason with God. Since God is so great, how could someone so small and insignificant like you or me talk to Him, negotiate with Him or even reason with Him? But it seems we can also negotiate with Him as Abraham did.

COME NOW, AND LET US REASON TOGETHER, saith the Lord: though your sins be as scarlet, they shall be as white as snow; though they be red like crimson, they shall be as wool.

Isaiah 1:18

PRODUCE YOUR CAUSE, saith the Lord; BRING FORTH
YOUR STRONG REASONS, saith the King of Jacob.

Isaiah 41:21

Abraham's Famous Negotiation

Abraham is known for a famous prayer in which he negotiated
for the lives of an entire city. He discussed with the Lord and
reasoned with Him about why He should not destroy the city of
Sodom and Gomorrah. It was Abraham's famous negotiations and
reasoning with God that almost saved Sodom and Gomorrah. Even
though God agreed to all of Abraham's terms, they were unable to
find ten righteous men.

Peradventure there be fifty righteous within the city: wilt
thou also destroy and not spare the place for the fifty
righteous that are therein?

That be far from thee to do after this manner, to slay the
righteous with the wicked: and that the righteous should be
as the wicked, that be far from thee: Shall not the Judge of all
the earth do right?

And the Lord said, If I find in Sodom fifty righteous within
the city, then I will spare all the place for their sakes.

And Abraham answered and said, Behold now, I have taken
upon me to speak unto the Lord, which am but dust and
ashes:

Peradventure there shall lack five of the fifty righteous: wilt
thou destroy all the city for lack of five? And he said, If I find
there forty and five, I will not destroy it.

And he spake unto him yet again, and said, Peradventure
there shall be forty found there. And he said, I will not do it
for forty's sake.

And he said unto him, Oh let not the Lord be angry, and I will
speak: Peradventure there shall thirty be found there. And he
said, I will not do it, if I find thirty there.

And he said, Behold now, I have taken upon me to speak unto the Lord: Peradventure there shall be twenty found there. And he said, I will not destroy it for twenty's sake.

And he said, Oh let not the Lord be angry, and I will speak yet but this once: Peradventure ten shall be found there. And he said, I will not destroy it for ten's sake.

Genesis 18:24-32

A Pastor Negotiates

I remember the testimony of a man who was working on a project and fell from a height into some machinery. He was rushed to the hospital and remained in a coma for some days. His pastor was called for and he prayed for him in the hospital. A few months later, this man was discharged from the hospital and gave a testimony in church.

He described how he had actually died during the experience in the hospital and gone to Heaven. It was so beautiful and he did not want to come back to earth. He vividly described the scenes of Heaven to the enthusiastic congregation. At a point he met the Lord Jesus and told Him how glad he was to be in Heaven.

But Jesus told him, "I am sorry, you will have to go back!"

"No, no, no, he exclaimed. "I will never go back to earth. I am so happy to be here."

But Jesus insisted, "I am sorry you will have to go back. Your pastor is not allowing you to stay in Heaven."

"How can my pastor not allow me to stay in Heaven," He shouted. "I will never go back to earth. Once I am here, I am here." Then Jesus turned and showed him a sort of curtain, which he pulled aside. The man suddenly heard his pastor's voice as he was praying in the hospital. His pastor was saying, "I am not going to let him die. Lord I refuse to let him die. He has a family and he needs to be on earth."

The man was amazed and he realized that his pastor's prayers and negotiations were powerfully effective in Heaven.

Everyone was awestruck by the man's testimony. Everyone realized how real and powerful prayers were.

Do not be baffled by this great mystery that a human being can negotiate with God. God has told us to come and reason with Him. I know it sounds fantastic that you can actually discuss issues with God and explain to Him why you want a beloved, a husband, a wife or a child. You can explain to God why you want your church to grow or why you want your business to increase. It is time to pray and negotiate with your heavenly Father for what you need.

7.   Mysteriously, it seems that even though prophets are men with disgraceful passions, thoughts and feelings, God seems to pay attention to their prayers.

Elias was A MAN SUBJECT TO LIKE PASSIONS as we are, and he prayed earnestly that it might not rain: and it rained not on the earth by the space of three years and six months.

James 5:17

Confess your faults one to another, and pray one for another, that ye may be healed. The effectual fervent prayer of a righteous man availeth much.

James 5:16

Elijah was a man who suffered from the same raging human passions that you have. All of us will acknowledge that our human passions are so disgraceful and embarrassing. And yet, God answers the prayers of people who have these feelings. From today do not be confused about your feelings! You are just like Elijah, a man with like passions. You are a human being and God listens to the prayers of frail human beings just like you. Mysteriously, God is open to your prayers in spite of the disgraceful passions and feelings you experience. Is that not good news?

8.   Mysteriously, it seems that God answers prayers immediately.

Unlike poorly run government offices that may not respond promptly to our needs, God listens to our prayers and answers them immediately. Somehow, there is a feeling that God really takes His time to answer prayers. It is like He dilly-dallies about the things we need. We get the feeling that He may or may not do what we really want. However, different accounts in the Bible show that God does answer prayer immediately. Notice the immediate answers that Hezekiah and Daniel had to their prayers.

a.   Hezekiah's immediate answer

Hezekiah prayed for mercy and long life. God answered his prayer and sent the prophet right back to his house. Before the prophet could cross the courtyard the answer to the prayer had come. Years ago, we could probably not have understood this phenomenon of instant answers from a very distant location. But now, with the advent of mobile phones we can understand how a message can reach Australia in a matter of seconds and a response can be received in a matter of seconds.

> In those days was Hezekiah sick unto death. And the prophet Isaiah the son of Amoz came to him, and said unto him, Thus saith the Lord, Set thine house in order; for thou shalt die, and not live.
>
> THEN HE TURNED HIS FACE TO THE WALL, AND PRAYED UNTO THE LORD, SAYING,
>
> I beseech thee, O Lord, remember now how I have walked before thee in truth and with a perfect heart, and have done that which is good in thy sight. And Hezekiah wept sore.
>
> And it came to pass, AFORE ISAIAH WAS GONE OUT INTO THE MIDDLE COURT, that the word of the Lord came to him, saying,
>
> Turn again, and tell Hezekiah the captain of my people, Thus saith the Lord, the God of David thy father, I have heard thy

prayer, I have seen thy tears: behold, I will heal thee: on the third day thou shalt go up unto the house of the Lord.

2 Kings 20:1-5

b. Daniel's instant response

In the third year of Cyrus king of Persia a thing was revealed unto Daniel, whose name was called Belteshazzar; and the thing was true, but the time appointed was long: and he understood the thing, and had understanding of the vision.

> In those days I DANIEL WAS MOURNING THREE FULL WEEKS.
>
> Daniel 10:1-2

> Then said he unto me, Fear not, Daniel: for FROM THE FIRST DAY that thou didst set thine heart to understand, and to chasten thyself before thy God, THY WORDS WERE HEARD, and I am come for thy words.
>
> Daniel 10:12

Daniel also received an instant response to his prayers. Daniel actually prayed for three whole weeks. When the angel appeared to him, he informed Daniel that his prayers were actually heard on the first day he prayed. There was no need to worry even when it seemed that God was delaying. God had answered immediately!

c. Elijah's instant response

Elijah also prayed to God and was heard immediately. He needed the fire at a particular time to make a point to the prophets of Baal. God honoured him and answered him immediately.

> And it came to pass *at the time* of the offering of the *evening* sacrifice, that Elijah the prophet came near, and said, Lord God of Abraham, Isaac, and of Israel, let it be known this day that thou art God in Israel, and that I am thy servant, and that I have done all these things at thy word.
>
> HEAR ME, O LORD, HEAR ME, that this people may know that thou art the Lord God, and that thou hast turned

their heart back again.THEN THE FIRE OF THE LORD FELL, and consumed the burnt sacrifice, and the wood, and the stones, and the dust, and licked up the water that was in the trench.

1 Kings 18:36-38

Chapter 3

What Happens When
You Do Not Pray

1. WHEN YOU DO NOT PRAY YOUR LIFE IS DIRECTED BY HAPPENSTANCE.

What is *happenstance*? *Happenstance* is another word for chance, circumstances, good luck, bad luck, good fortune, misfortune, quirks, serendipity and twists of fate.

Unfortunately, chance, circumstances, good luck, bad luck, good fortune, misfortune, quirks are also governed by other factors. The so-called events of *chance* are actually governed by natural things and also by spiritual things.

How Natural Factors Govern Chance

In the natural, we know of many things that look like chance but are actually not. For instance, I was once amazed to hear of an author who had been given a contract to write a bestselling book.

I asked, "How do they know his book will be a bestseller?"

Then I found out that many bestselling books are designated as such even before they are written. I found out that many so-called bestselling books are not bestsellers but are presented as such to the public even before they are written.

Some publishers have even been known to buy back thousands of copies of books they have published so as to create the impression that the book is a bestseller.

To everyone's amazement, it comes out in the news once in a while that the winners of some soccer matches, cricket matches are determined even before the match is played. What looks like a fluke is not a fluke at all! Many apparently lucky events are actually being orchestrated and implemented by unseen human forces.

There was a time I would go to the horse races every Saturday. Initially, I thought the best horse would win the race. Later on, I thought the luckiest horse would be the winner. But with time I found out that neither the luckiest nor the best was predestined to win. There were actually people determining who would win or lose.

I found out that the jockeys were given instructions by the owners of the horses to hold back their horse and prevent it from running as fast as it could. Sometimes, the jockeys were asked to ensure that they came last in a race. This was all in order to get their horses to be demoted to a lower division where there were inferior horses and where they would carry less weight. Indeed, to my shock the races were fixed in order to make certain gamblers win more money.

If events that are apparently governed by luck and chance are actually controlled by people's decisions then perhaps we can conclude that there is probably nothing like luck or chance.

How Spiritual Factors Govern Chance

Spiritual factors also govern what we call chance. In a famous story about the death of King Ahab, we see how he died by an apparent stroke of bad luck. The king was fully disguised. No one knew who he was. In spite of that, an arrow which was shot out at random hit the king at a joint in the armour. What a stroke of coincidence! Indeed, but it was not really a stroke of coincidence! There had been a meeting in the spirit realm and an evil spirit had been commissioned to get Ahab to go to the battle where he would die. What was apparently a fluke was determined by a decision of evil spirits. Read it for yourself.

The Planning of the Death of Ahab by Evil Spirits

And he said, Hear thou therefore the word of the LORD: I saw the LORD sitting on his throne, and all the host of heaven standing by him on his right hand and on his left.

And the LORD said, WHO SHALL PERSUADE AHAB, THAT HE MAY GO UP AND FALL AT RAMOTHGILEAD? And one said on this manner, and another said on that manner.

AND THERE CAME FORTH A SPIRIT, AND STOOD BEFORE THE LORD, AND SAID, I WILL PERSUADE HIM.

And the LORD said unto him, wherewith? And he said, I will go forth, and I will be a lying spirit in the mouth of all his prophets. And he said, Thou shalt persuade him, and prevail also: go forth, and do so.

Now therefore, behold, the LORD hath put a lying spirit in the mouth of all these thy prophets, and the LORD hath spoken evil concerning thee.

1 Kings 22:19-23

The Death of Ahab by Apparent Coincidence

The king of Israel said to Jehoshaphat, "I will enter the battle in disguise, but you wear your royal robes." So THE KING OF ISRAEL DISGUISED HIMSELF and went into battle.

Now the king of Aram had ordered his thirty-two chariot commanders, "Do not fight with anyone, small or great, except the king of Israel."

When the chariot commanders saw Jehoshaphat, they thought, "Surely this is the king of Israel." So they turned to attack him, but when Jehoshaphat cried out,the chariot commanders saw that he was not the king of Israel and stopped pursuing him.

But SOMEONE DREW HIS BOW AT RANDOM and HIT THE KING OF ISRAEL BETWEEN THE SECTIONS OF HIS ARMOR. The king told his chariot driver, "Wheel around and get me out of the fighting. I've been wounded."

All day long the battle raged, and the king was propped up in his chariot facing the Arameans. The blood from his wound ran onto the floor of the chariot, and that evening he died.

1 Kings 22:30-35, NIV

This story reveals the reality that good luck and bad luck is not as random as it may appear to be. Ahab did not die from a sad and bad stroke of evil coincidence. When the events were played out they may have looked like chance but they were happenings that were orchestrated by evil spirits.

2. WHEN YOU DO NOT PRAY, YOUR LIFE IS GOVERNED BY THE MAJOR CURSES IN THIS WORLD.

The course of this world is determined largely by three curses. These three curses were instituted at the beginning of time and are recorded in the Bible. Most people's lives play out according to these three major curses. They are the curse on Adam, the curse on Eve and the curse on Ham.

The curse on Adam is a punishment on all men for Adam's disobedience. It ensures that men suffer and sweat in this life for prosperity and for their existence.

The curse on Eve is a punishment on all women for Eve's disobedience. It ensures that women are drawn helplessly to men and suffer through this inexorable attraction. It also ensures that women suffer through the act of marriage and having children.

The curse on Ham is a punishment on Ham, the dark son of Noah. This punishment explains the difficult conditions under which black people struggle all over the world. It is a curse that is played out in every continent on this world. Black people

28

everywhere have the lowest levels of wealth, health, education and standards of living. It can be the only explanation for the state of the black man in every part of the world.

How Does Prayer Affect These Curses?

When you do not pray and intercede, your life will follow a stereotyped pattern determined by these curses. Through prayer and intercession, you receive wisdom. A large part of your prayer must be for wisdom.

Curses are always made more bearable through wisdom! Curses are defeated and minimised through prayers for wisdom. Wisdom will be given to you to navigate a different and better course of life. When you get wisdom, riches, honour, length of days and many blessings arrive in your life and overrule the effect of the curse on man.

"Happy is the man that findeth wisdom, and the man that getteth understanding.

For the merchandise of it is better than the merchandise of silver, and the gain thereof than fine gold.

She is more precious than rubies: and all the things thou canst desire are not to be compared unto her.

Length of days is in her right hand; and in her left hand riches and honour" (Proverbs 3:13-16).

Women are equally helped by wisdom. They are delivered from blindly following men and living their lives with one heartbreak after another. Through wisdom, which is medical science, childbearing is not as destructive and harmful to women.

The black man who historically has been at the bottom of the charts rises through the gift of wisdom. Black people are able to rise above servanthood through wisdom. The black man will not be the lowest and the least anymore when he walks in the wisdom of God.

So prayer, especially for wisdom, will greatly change the course of a person's life and deliver him from the curses that are directing and governing the masses. Without prayer, you will fall into the patterns that all men, all women and all black people experience.

3. **WHEN YOU DO NOT PRAY, YOUR LIFE IN THIS WORLD WILL BE GOVERNED PURELY BY THE GOD OR CONTROLLER OF THIS WORLD.**

In the Bible, Satan is called the god of this world.

In whom the god of this world hath blinded the minds of them which believe not, lest the light of the glorious gospel of Christ, who is the image of God, should shine unto them.

2 Corinthians 4:4

The god of this world is the ruler and governor of the events and circumstances in the world. The god of this world, Satan, is therefore directing the affairs of this world.

Even though God is the creator of the whole world, there is a sense in which Satan is controlling and guiding the affairs in our world. It is easy to see that Satan is the god of this world because he directs this world into the wars, conflicts and the many countless sorrows and tragedies of humanity.

It is because Satan has great influence and control in this world that he offered Jesus the kingdoms of the world in the temptation. That is the reason why it was a temptation, because Satan actually had the kingdoms of this world under his control. He was offering them to Jesus if Jesus would bow down.

Again, the devil taketh him up into an exceeding high mountain, and sheweth him all the kingdoms of the world, and the glory of them;

And saith unto him, All these things will I give thee, if thou wilt fall down and worship me.

Matthew 4:8-9

When you do not pray, you do not call on God to intervene in the life you are leading on this earth. Whether you like it or not, the life you have on this earth is affected by the head of state of your country. In the same way, our lives on earth are greatly affected by the one who controls the kingdoms of the earth.

Almighty God expects you to invite Him to legally intervene in the events and circumstances of your life here. If there is no intervention, things will go a certain way. In the book of Ecclesiastes, there is a prediction that all those born in a certain kingdom will be poor.

> For out of prison he cometh to reign; whereas also HE THAT IS BORN IN HIS KINGDOM BECOMETH POOR.
>
> Ecclesiastes 4:14

Indeed, all those born in certain parts of the world are usually poor. Unless there is some special intervention, if you live in certain countries you will be poor.

Indeed, we all need the special intervention of the Lord because we are working and dwelling in a world ruled by a very wicked being. Do you now understand why the world is full of sorrow and pain?

How can you live in this world without calling on God to intervene and to step into your life under this terrible, wicked, fallen enemy of God? It is time to pray and commit yourself to God. It is time to deliver yourself out of the patterns and stereotypes which Satan has prepared for those who live in this world.

4. WHEN YOU DO NOT PRAY, YOU DO NOT INTERVENE OR MODIFY EVENTS THAT TAKE PLACE IN THE SPIRIT REALM.

Spiritual beings and spiritual events cause things to take place in the natural. In the book of Revelation you will see how seals were opened, trumpets were blown and bowls were emptied onto the earth. Each seal that was opened and each trumpet that was blown triggered events on earth.

When you pray, you enter the spirit realm and affect what is going on there. He that speaks in an unknown tongue speaketh not unto men but in the spirit (realm) he speaks mysteries. In other words, prayer is operating in the spirit realm.

Read it for yourself and you will see how the removal of spiritual seals in the spirit realm triggered off the major events in our physical world. White, black, red and pale horses began cantering in the spirit bringing about major changes on earth. Every time you pray, you are doing something spiritual! When you pray, you are interrupting spiritual events and affecting what happens in the spirit realm.

And I saw when the Lamb opened one of the seals, and I heard, as it were the noise of thunder, one of the four beasts saying, Come and see.

And I saw, and behold a white horse: and he that sat on him had a bow; and a crown was given unto him: and he went forth conquering, and to conquer.

And when he had opened the second seal, I heard the second beast say, Come and see.

And there went out another horse that was red: and power was given to him that sat thereon to take peace from the earth, and that they should kill one another: and there was given unto him a great sword.

And when he had opened the third seal, I heard the third beast say, Come and see. And I beheld, and lo a black horse; and he that sat on him had a pair of balances in his hand.

And I heard a voice in the midst of the four beasts say, A measure of wheat for a penny, and three measures of barley for a penny; and see thou hurt not the oil and the wine.

And when he had opened the fourth seal, I heard the voice of the fourth beast say, Come and see.

And I looked, and behold a pale horse: and his name that sat on him was Death, and Hell followed with him. And power was given unto them over the fourth part of the earth, to kill with sword, and with hunger, and with death, and with the beasts of the earth.

Revelation 6:1-8

5. WHEN YOU DO NOT PRAY, YOUR LIFE IS GOVERNED BY THE WICKEDNESS OF MEN.

And we know that ... the whole world lieth in wickedness.

1 John 5:19

The evil planted in men is growing. The will of man is not the will of God. The will of man is often the will of Satan. The whole world lieth in wickedness. Your life cannot be governed by the wickedness of men. Evil is multiplying and the depravity of men is becoming more pronounced. Anyone who is successful is envied by those around him.

Again, I considered all travail, and every right work, that for this a man is envied of his neighbour. This is also vanity and vexation of spirit.

Ecclesiastes 4:4

This unfortunate state of the human heart gives rise to the terrible evils of our world. No matter how much good you do, men will hate you, envy you and dislike you. That will be your reward for all your contributions to society. It is only when you are dead and gone that statues will be built in your honour.

This is one of the important reasons why prayer must go up on your behalf. The wickedness of humanity can overwhelm you and overpower your life.

What did Jesus Christ encounter when He came into this world? Human jealousy, fears, wickedness, betrayal and conflict! These human characteristics have taken over and determined the course of events in this world.

This is why Jesus prayed in the garden of Gethsemane. There were many forces that were working to drive Him to His death before it was His time. The Pharisees envied Him. Many Jews hated Him. The Romans despised Him. The soldiers desired His money. Judas was greedy and disloyal. The executioners were full of wickedness and had no feeling. Pontius Pilate wanted political power. The wife of Pontius Pilate was full of fears. In short, there are many strong forces raging and influencing events. The strongest of these forces would carry the day.

But the life of Jesus was too important to be governed by the hatred, jealousies, fears and ambitions of evil men. The life and ministry of Jesus would be governed by God and not by human nature.

This is why Jesus went to the Garden of Gethsemane for so many hours. He prayed that the will of God would be done. His trial could have gone in many different directions.

It is possible that all those healed by Jesus would have come to testify that He was a good person.

The centurion whose servant was healed could have shown up at the trial and turned the tide of events.

The masses could have been offended and afraid of Pilate's washing his hands on them.

The crowds could have rejected the release of Barabbas and requested for the release of Christ.

Judas could have changed his mind about betraying Jesus and repented from his bad ideas.

Jesus Himself could have opted out of the cross, because of bodily pains and extreme suffering! He would then not have died on the cross because the suffering would have been too much to bear.

This is why Jesus prayed so long and so hard in the Garden of Gethsemane. He wanted the will of God to be done. He prayed that the Father would intervene so that the will of God would be done and not the will of man. He prayed so that His life would not be governed by man's jealousies, greed, ambition, hatred, forgetfulness, disloyalty, ingratitude and wickedness.

If you do not pray, your life will be governed and controlled by the will of men. Do you want your life to follow the will of God or the will of man? The disloyalties, fears, jealousies, greed and hatred of men will unravel your nice plans for life and bring you to a place you never planned to be.

Give yourself over to the will of God through prayer. Pray until God's will is done. The opposite of God's will is man's will. Man's will is often guided by Satan. Jesus rebuked Peter for being against the cross. He told him, "You like the things of men; you want things to go the way of men." Jesus pointed out to him that the will of men was the will of Satan.

Then Peter took him, and began to rebuke him, saying, Be it far from thee, Lord: this shall not be unto thee.

But he turned, and said unto Peter, Get thee behind me, Satan: thou art an offence unto me: for THOU SAVOUREST NOT THE THINGS THAT BE OF GOD, but THOSE THAT BE OF MEN."

Matthew 16:22-23

Chapter 4

How to Talk to a Great Person

P rayer is talking to a great person called Jehovah: I am that I
am! He is the greatest of all. He is the creator of Heaven and
earth. He is the Lord of Lords. He knows the beginning and
the end! There is none like Him! No one else can touch our lives
that way that He does! How great is our God and how great is His
name!

Whenever we pray, we come before the great and everlasting
God. There must be a way to speak to Him properly. We must
learn how to speak to this great God. A simple way of learning how
to pray is to learn how to speak to a great person. Indeed, many of
the principles that must be used when talking to a great person are
the principles that are used in prayer.

What are the principles you must have in mind when you are
speaking to a great person?

1. DO NOT ASK FOR OR MENTION YOUR NEEDS AT THE BEGINNING OF YOUR INTERACTION.

You may have a legitimate need and the important person may be
the right person who can solve your problem. The need you have
may be something very noble and very right.

But the timing of the mention of your need is critical. It is very
tempting to ask an important person for what you need. You may
know that the important person has what you need. You may also
know that he can easily supply your needs. But you must control
yourself and not mention your needs to this great person.

Many years ago, whilst living in London, I was really broke and in need. Every time I met an uncle or a relative I immediately wanted to inform them of my need for a few pounds. I could see that they had lots of pounds. I could see that they did not know that I did not have any money. I could see that they were completely unaware of my dire situation. Oh how I was tempted to blurt out, "Please give me fifty pounds." It is natural to want to tell great people what you need when you see them.

But when Jesus taught us to pray, He taught us not to mention our needs first. Our needs are to be mentioned much later in the discussion, if at all. Many years ago, on my first interaction with a great pastor, Yonggi Cho, I invited him to come to Ghana to dedicate my church. But that was a mistake. He flatly refused and I left the meeting dejected and depressed. He cited some bad experiences he had had with other African pastors. I could not blame him because he did not even know me. The dedication of my church was thrown out of the window.

However, after years of relating with him, he himself decided to come to Ghana at his own expense and dedicate my church. There are also many other things I have asked him for which I easily receive. I just send an email and I get a positive answer from him.

I learnt the valuable lesson of not mentioning my needs at the beginning of a relationship or a discussion. Jesus taught us to pray after this manner or in this pattern. The pattern is clear; bring up your needs later on.

AFTER THIS MANNER THEREFORE PRAY ye: Our Father which art in heaven, Hallowed be thy name. Thy kingdom come. Thy will be done in earth, as it is in heaven.

Give us this day our daily bread. And forgive us our debts, as we forgive our debtors.

And lead us not into temptation, but deliver us from evil: For thine is the kingdom, and the power, and the glory, for ever. Amen.

Matthew 6:9-13

37

2. DO NOT ASK FOR OR MENTION YOUR DESIRES AT THE BEGINNING OF YOUR INTERACTION.

When Esther, the Queen, went to see the king to make request for the lives of her people the Jews, she wisely used this time-tested strategy of talking to an important person. She did not immediately ask for her desires. She avoided the mistake that many people make when they desire help or assistance from a great person. She did not ask the king for what she wanted until the second night of interaction.

She just stayed in his company, chatted with him and enjoyed his presence. On the second day, it was the king himself who began to press her to say what she needed and what she wanted. Read it for yourself:

> So the king and Haman came to banquet with Esther the queen.

> And the king said again unto Esther on THE SECOND DAY at the banquet of wine, WHAT IS THY PETITION, queen Esther? and it shall be granted thee: and what is thy request? and it shall be performed, even to the half of the kingdom.

> Then Esther the queen answered and said, If I have found favour in thy sight, O king, and if it please the king, let my life be given me at my petition, and my people at my request:

> Esther 7:1-3

Avoid this great mistake of saying what you want at the beginning of your interaction with a great person. Many people have destroyed their relationships and ended their conversations with important people by asking for a laptop, a bicycle or even for money.

If they had learned just how to talk with an important person without bringing up their needs or desires, they would probably have developed a strong close relationship and one day received their desires, anyway.

3. LEARN HOW TO GENUINELY TALK ABOUT THE GREATNESS OF THE GREAT PERSON.

If you talk about the greatness of a great person in a way that is not genuine, you irritate the great person. Great people can see through the words of a flatterer. We are to start our interaction with the Lord by thanking Him, honouring Him and praising Him. Every important person will warm up to you when you say nice things to him.

One day whilst chatting with a rich man, I asked him whether he supported a political party. He laughed and said to me, "I once supported a political party and gave them a lot of money but I do not do that any more."

"Why not?" I asked

He laughed and said, "Some years ago, some politicians came to me and spoke nice words to me. They told me I was one of the wisest people in the country."

Then he continued, "Being so foolish, I swallowed this story and believed that I was one of the wisest people in the country. So I gave them a lot of money." Nowadays, I do not believe whether they say I am the wisest, the most intelligent or most clever person in the world. I just do not give my money away."

You see, the politician had spoken wisely to this great man and told him nice things that he liked to hear. Everyone would like to hear that he is the wisest person in the country. The politician had learnt the art of talking to a great person. God is equally impressed when we approach him with praise, worship and honour that come from our hearts.

Of course, God can see through hypocrisy and empty words.

"But when ye pray, use not vain repetitions, as the heathen do: for they think that they shall be heard for their much speaking" (Matthew 6:7).

Indeed, we must learn the art of coming to God with words of genuine praise and honour. We must tell the Lord words that we believe are true. We must enter His gates with thanksgiving and his courts with praise. That is how to start talking to a great God – with thanksgiving, with praise and with honour.

Enter into his gates with thanksgiving, and into his courts with praise: be thankful unto him, and bless his name.

Psalm 100:4

4. **LEARN HOW TO STAY COMFORTABLY IN THE PRESENCE OF AN IMPORTANT PERSON FOR A LONG TIME WITHOUT BEING NERVOUS.**

The ability of a person to stay in the same place with a great person without wishing to leave or checking the time is an important thing. Great people notice those who are fidgety and uncomfortable in their presence. No one wants to be "unwanted". I do not want to be in the presence of people who do not want to be with me. I do not like being with people who are constantly looking at their watches and wishing for their time in my presence to end.

You can learn to be comfortable in the presence of God by playing music or preaching messages. These create an atmosphere which makes it possible for you to stay comfortably in the presence of God for a long time.

Also, you can put on videos and play church services from the very beginning and to the very end. This creates an atmosphere where you can stay in His presence for even longer periods. Somehow, you become more relaxed, less fidgety and less in a hurry to run out of His presence. God loves people who are not in a hurry to leave. God loves to talk to people who are not in a hurry to go somewhere else.

Rest in the LORD, and wait patiently for him: fret not thyself because of him who prospereth in his way, because of the man who bringeth wicked devices to pass.

Psalms 37:7

But they that wait upon the Lord shall renew their strength; they shall mount up with wings as eagles; they shall run, and not be weary; and they shall walk, and not faint.

Isaiah 40:31

5. LEARN HOW TO TALK TO THE IMPORTANT PERSON ABOUT THINGS HE HAS SAID OR WRITTEN.

If ye abide in me, and MY WORDS ABIDE IN YOU, ye shall ask what ye will, and it shall be done unto you.

John 15:7

How impressive it is when you speak to someone who knows what you have said or written. Make sure you remind the important person about things that he has said by quoting statements he has made before.

You reveal your intelligence when you are able to play back the important person's words. You reveal your understanding of important wisdom.

As an author, I am always impressed when I meet people who know what I have written and what I have said. The easiest way to get into conversation with an important person is to start talking about the many things that the important person has ever said.

I once spoke to a little girl in a church service to see if she could maintain a conversation with me. I was amazed as she quoted different things that I had said in the past. She quoted from my book on The Art of Hearing. She told me that I had written about twelve kinds of voices which were important for every Christian. I was amazed at her knowledge of my different teachings. She kept talking to me for an hour and I warmed up to her because I was impressed that she knew me so well.

Jesus said, "If my words abide in you, you shall ask what you will and it will be done unto you." The more you know about what God has said the more you will be able to speak to the Lord. The more you know about what God has said, the more you will be able to speak to Him intelligently and properly.

When you know the words that God has spoken, you will speak with the Lord according to His own words.

And this is the confidence that we have in him, that, if we ASK ANY THING ACCORDING TO HIS WILL, he heareth us:

And if we know that he hear us, whatsoever we ask, we know that we have the petitions that we desired of him.

1 John 5:14-15

6.   LEARN HOW TO TALK ABOUT THE IMPORTANT PERSON'S GREATEST PURPOSE AND GOALS IN LIFE.

In the natural, the purpose of most great people in this life hinges around things like business, politics and the events of the day. If you cannot talk to a great person about these subjects you are not likely to be able to stay for long in his presence.

In the same way, God has great interests. His great interests are His eternal work and His eternal purpose. The more you are able to talk to God about His eternal work and His eternal purpose, the more you will have to say in prayer.

Matthew 28:18 encapsulates the great interest that the Lord Jesus has in the earth. His great purpose is saving all the nations by building churches, planting churches and teaching the Word of God.

If you are involved in building the church, you will have a lot to talk to God about. You can be with Him for hours as you pray for His will to be done in the church.

This is why pastors and those who work for God have more to pray about. If you want to improve your prayer life begin to work for God. The more you work for God, the more you will have to pray about.

Go ye therefore, and teach all nations, baptizing them in the name of the Father, and of the Son, and of the Holy Ghost:

Teaching them to observe all things whatsoever I have commanded you: and, lo, I am with you alway, even unto the end of the world. Amen.

Matthew 28:19-20

Jesus Christ spent three hours praying in the garden of Gethsemane for the will of God to be done. Anyone who works towards the will of God being done will spend hours in the presence of God. Jesus spent hours putting His life in the hands of God and entrusting Himself to the will of God. He was amazed that up and coming pastors like Peter and John could not do that for at least one hour. Peter and the other disciples were just students. They were not yet working for God. It is Jesus who was actively working for the Lord. That is why He could not sleep that night. The students slept but the worker stayed up and prayed to the Lord for three hours. This is the pattern you find all over the church. The workers pray and the members sleep! Are you a worker? When you become a genuine worker you will pray for many hours.

And he cometh unto the disciples, and findeth them asleep, and saith unto Peter, What, could ye not watch with me one hour?

Matthew 26:40

7.   LEARN HOW TO TALK ABOUT WHAT A GREAT PERSON LOVES.

Great people love different things. Some great people love soccer. Some great people love golf. Some great people love tennis. Many great people love money, stocks and bonds.

These things may not be the purpose of the great person in this life but he loves them and he loves to talk about them. If you have nothing to say about golf, you may not be able to sustain an interesting conversation with the great person. If you have nothing to say about business, politics, money, stocks and bonds, you may have very little to say to the great person.

In the same way, there are things that God loves.

What does God love? God so loved the world that He gave His Son. God loves sinners. God loves evangelism. You will have to learn to talk to God about the lost people in the world and the sinners that He came to die for.

People do not pray for long because they do not pray for souls to be saved. They have no interest in souls and therefore they have no interest in what God loves. Because of this, they are unable to sustain a conversation with the Lord.

For God so loved the world, that he gave his only begotten Son, that whosoever believeth in him should not perish, but have everlasting life.

John 3:16

For the Son of man is come to seek and to save that which was lost.

Luke 19:10

People do not pray for long because they are not interceding for those who are about to go to Hell and burn in the lake of fire. All Christians who spend a long time calling on God for the lost will have a lot to pray about and will spend hours in the presence of God.

Abraham spent hours negotiating with God about the people of Sodom and Gomorrah who were about to be burnt in the fire of judgement. He was interceding for lost people. That is why his prayer is recorded as one of the famous prayers in the Word of God.

8. LEARN TO ASK FOR WHAT THE GREAT PERSON THINKS YOU NEED.

Do not ask for things the important person has no intention of doing. Do not waste your time asking for things that are clearly not in His will or plan. You must analyse and judge what you think is the great person's wish and will for you. That is what you must ask for. Ask for what the great person thinks you need. That is what you will get. And then you will begin to get other things. We can glean the will and the wishes of God from the Bible. There are many things that are clear that He wishes and wills for us. Those are the things we must spend our time asking for. It is far more productive to ask for things which are specifically laid out than to make strange requests which the great person has no intention of giving you.

And this is the confidence that we have in him, that, if we ask any thing according to his will, he heareth us:

1 John 5: 14

Most rich and great people do not think that poor people need money! Most rich nations do not think that poor and developing nations need money per se. The presidents of America and Europe think that poor and developing countries need democracy and the rule of law more than anything else. They think that poor nations need to do away with corruption. They also think that poor nations need good education and good health.

Have you not noticed that when rich countries are assisting poor nations they give help in specific areas? They help with elections, they help with education and they help with health. But they do not help by donating presidential jets and presidential helicopters.

God does not think we need money too. God thinks that we need wisdom and the Holy Spirit.

As you read through the Bible, you will discover that there are very few prayer topics that are given to us. These are the most important things to pray for. They are what God thinks we need. God thinks that we need the Holy Spirit. Jesus promised us the Holy Spirit to help and empower us. When you ask for these things you will receive them. When you ask for presidential helicopters you will not receive them.

If a son shall ask bread of any of you that is a father, will he give him a stone? Or if he ask a fish, will he for a fish give him a serpent?

Or if he shall ask an egg, will he offer him a scorpion?

If ye then, being evil, know how to give good gifts unto your children: how much more shall your heavenly Father give the Holy Spirit to them that ask him?

Luke 11:11-13

There are many reasons why Jesus told us to pray for the Holy Spirit. The Holy Spirit is God and He will help us to live a supernatural, holy and upright life. Instead of wasting time to pray for things that will never be answered, let us start asking for things that can and will be answered.

Praying for wisdom and revelation is one of most important things to pray for. It is one of the prayers God will answer. It is one of the requests God is impressed by. This is one of the reasons why Solomon is considered to be wise. When God asked him what he wanted he asked for wisdom. Through wisdom he had everything else given to him. God was so impressed with his prayer topic that He gave him everything else that he did not ask for.

In Gibeon the LORD appeared to Solomon in a dream by night: and GOD SAID, ASK WHAT I SHALL GIVE THEE.

And Solomon said, Thou hast shewed unto thy servant David my father great mercy, according as he walked before thee in truth, and in righteousness, and in uprightness of heart with thee; and thou hast kept for him this great kindness, that thou hast given him a son to sit on his throne, as it is this day.

And now, O Lord my God, thou hast made thy servant king instead of David my father: and I am but a little child: I know not how to go out or come in.

And thy servant is in the midst of thy people which thou hast chosen, a great people, that cannot be numbered nor counted for multitude.

GIVE THEREFORE THY SERVANT AN UNDERSTANDING HEART to judge thy people, that I may discern between good and bad: for who is able to judge this thy so great a people?

AND THE SPEECH PLEASED THE LORD, THAT SOLOMON HAD ASKED THIS THING.

And God said unto him, Because thou hast asked this thing, and hast not asked for thyself long life; neither hast asked riches for thyself, nor hast asked the life of thine enemies; but hast asked for thyself understanding to discern judgment;

Behold, I have done according to thy words: lo, I have given thee a wise and an understanding heart; so that there was none like thee before thee, neither after thee shall any arise like unto thee.

And I HAVE ALSO GIVEN THEE THAT WHICH THOU HAST NOT ASKED, both riches, and honour: so that there shall not be any among the kings like unto thee all thy days.

1 Kings 3:5-13

Chapter 5

How You Can Be Helped by Praying in Tongues

Likewise the Spirit also helpeth our infirmities: for WE KNOW NOT WHAT WE SHOULD PRAY FOR AS WE OUGHT: but the Spirit itself maketh intercession for us with groanings which cannot be uttered.

Romans 8:26

Perhaps your greatest difficulty when you are talking to a great person is to *know what to talk about.* God understands this difficulty and limitation. He has therefore given us the gift of the Holy Spirit so that we can be helped in prayer. Even when you know all the principles and Scriptures about prayer, it is still difficult to know exactly what to pray for, as you ought. Remember that the Holy Spirit is called the helper and that is what He is here to do.

Throughout the New Testament, when people received the Holy Spirit a wonderful phenomenon was released. They began to speak in tongues that they did not understand. These tongues were heavenly languages. They were the tongues of men and the tongues of angels.

When you speak in tongues the Holy Spirit takes over and helps you to pray. You are the one speaking but the Holy Spirit is the one giving the utterance and the words (Acts 2:4).

These amazing tongues are also the sign of the great Holy Spirit indwelling believers. These wonderful tongues are characterized by stammering lips and stammering words.

You will often hear a lot of *ma ma ma* and *ba ba ba* when people speak in tongues. It is the stammering lips you are hearing.

For with stammering lips and another tongue will he speak to this people.

Isaiah 28:11

There are wonderful accounts of people receiving the Holy Spirit in the second, eighth, ninth, tenth and nineteenth chapters of the book of Acts. These accounts confirm to us that the commonest feature of receiving the Holy Spirit is speaking in tongues and prophesying.

As you read this book, I want you to have faith to receive the Holy Spirit and also to speak in tongues. When you speak in tongues you will receive assistance to spend a longer time in the presence of a great person. You will pray longer and harder. You will be assisted. You will be helped and you will be able to pray.

I now want to share with you some simple steps that will help you to receive the Holy Spirit and to speak in tongues.

How You Can Receive the Holy Spirit

1.   CONFESS YOUR SINS.

Confess your sins and ask God to forgive you for every mistake you have made. Once you are cleansed with the blood of Jesus you are ready to receive the Holy Ghost. The blood always comes before the oil. In the Old Testament, the priests were anointed with blood and then with oil. The blood cleanses you and makes you pure! Pure enough to receive the Holy Spirit! It is only after you are cleansed by the blood of Jesus from all sins that you can receive the Holy Spirit.

And the priest shall take some of the BLOOD of the trespass offering, and the priest shall put it upon the tip of the right ear of him that is to be cleansed, and upon the thumb of his right hand, and upon the great toe of his right foot: And the priest shall take some of the log of OIL, and pour it into the palm of his own left hand:

Leviticus 14:14-15

2.   ASK FOR THE HOLY SPIRIT.

Pray to the Father to receive the Holy Spirit. This is one of the only things Jesus taught us to ask for. The Holy Spirit will be given to you today when you ask for Him.

> If ye then, being evil, know how to give good gifts unto your children: how much more shall your heavenly Father give the Holy Spirit to them that ask him?
>
> Luke 11:13

3.   OPEN YOUR MOUTH AND SPEAK TO GOD.

When you pray for the Holy Spirit, you have to believe you have received the Holy Spirit. Then you must open your mouth and speak to God. When you do this, the Holy Spirit will take control of your tongue and you will begin to speak in tongues. Remember that God is not going to put a radio in your stomach that will start speaking on its own. You have to do the speaking and the Holy Spirit will give you utterance. Read the Scripture below and you will realise that you must speak while the Holy Spirit gives you utterance.

> And THEY were all filled with the Holy Ghost, and BEGAN TO SPEAK with other tongues, as THE SPIRIT GAVE THEM UTTERANCE.
>
> Acts 2:4

4.   GET AN ANOINTED SERVANT OF THE LORD TO LAY HANDS ON YOU SO THAT YOU CAN RECEIVE THE HOLY SPRIT.

All through the Bible, people received the Holy Spirit when anointed people laid hands on them. Even Simon the sorcerer recognized the power of laying on of hands. He noticed that when hands were laid on people they received the Holy Spirit and began to speak in tongues.

And WHEN SIMON SAW that through laying on of the apostles' hands the Holy Ghost was given, he offered them money, Saying, Give me also this power, that on whomsoever I lay hands, he may receive the Holy Ghost.

Acts 8:18-19

5. PRAY UNTIL YOU RECEIVE.

Expect to speak in tongues and pray for the Holy Spirit until you speak in tongues. Why should you be different from the people in the book of Acts? All those in the book of Acts received the Holy Spirit and spoke in tongues when they prayed for it. Expect to receive the same Holy Spirit and to speak in tongues in the same way! Asking for the Holy Spirit is asking in the will of God. Have confidence in your prayer for the Holy Spirit.

And THIS IS THE CONFIDENCE that we have in him, that, if we ask any thing according to his will, he heareth us: And if we know that he hear us, whatsoever we ask, we know that we have the petitions that we desired of him."

1 John 5:14-15

6. PERSISTENCE.

Do not give up if you do not receive the Holy Spirit and speak in tongues on the first occasion. Continue to pray for the Holy Spirit. Many rewards are promised to those who persist in prayer. I did not receive the Holy Spirit when I prayed the first time. Neither did I receive the Holy Spirit when hands were laid on me. I only received the Holy Spirit after several weeks of praying and persisting. Although I almost gave up, I never did and one day I began to speak in tongues when I was having my quiet time and lying on my bed. What a glorious day that was!

And He said to them, "Suppose one of you shall have a friend, and shall go to him at midnight, and say to him, 'Friend, lend me three loaves; for a friend of mine has come to me from a journey, and I have nothing to set before him';

51

And from inside he shall answer and say, 'Do not bother me; the door has already been shut and my children and I are in bed; I cannot get up and give you anything.'

I tell you, even though he will not get up and give him anything because he is his friend, YET BECAUSE OF HIS PERSISTENCE HE WILL GET UP AND GIVE HIM AS MUCH AS HE NEEDS."

Luke 11:5-8 (NASB)

7. LET THE RIVER FLOW.

When you start to speak in tongues do not stop quickly. The Holy Spirit is a river. Let the river flow! Continue to pray and let the river of tongues flow out of you. Initially when you start to speak in tongues it may sound funny or even silly.

When a river begins, it is a small unimpressive stream but as it grows it becomes broader, stronger and mightier. It is when the river is mighty that it becomes a blessing. Allow tongues to flow out of you like a mighty river. You will be blessed mightily when your tongues are a mighty river flowing out of your belly. Many people do not benefit from speaking in tongues because they do not allow the river of tongues to flow out of them properly.

He that believeth on me, as the scripture hath said, OUT OF HIS BELLY SHALL FLOW RIVERS of living water.

(But THIS SPAKE HE OF THE SPIRIT, which they that believe on him should receive: for the Holy Ghost was not yet given; because that Jesus was not yet glorified.)

John 7:38-39

Twenty-Five Benefits of Speaking in Tongues

I thank my God, I speak with tongues more than ye all.

1 Corinthians 14:18

What are the benefits of speaking in a language you do not understand?

Paul must have had a good reason for speaking in tongues so much. It was something that he did more than everyone he knew. The ability to pray in tongues is probably the best gift that God gave to Christians. I want to share with you why praying in tongues is so important even though you do not understand the language you are speaking. Each of the reasons has a biblical foundation and I want you to think about them for your own benefit.

Twenty-Five Reasons Why You Must Pray in Tongues

1. When you pray in tongues you charge yourself up like a battery (1 Corinthians 14:4).

2. When you pray in tongues you are immediately inspired by the Holy Spirit (Acts 2:4).

3. When you pray in tongues you pray from your heart (spirit) (1 Corinthians 14:14).

4. When you pray in tongues your prayer is dictated and directed by the Holy Spirit (Acts 2:4).

5. When you pray in tongues you operate instantly in the spirit realm (1 Corinthians 14:14).

6. When you pray in tongues other people do not understand what you are saying (1 Corinthians 14:14).

7. When you pray in tongues devils do not understand what you are saying (1 Corinthians 14:14).

8. When you pray in tongues you can hear the voice of the Spirit by interpreting your prayers (1 Corinthians 14:13).

9. When you pray in tongues you can pray for long hours like Jesus (Mark 1:35; Luke 6:12).

10. When you pray in tongues you can practise intercession for souls, families and nations (Ephesians 6:18).

11. When you pray in tongues you can speak to yourself and to God. This helps you to concentrate on God everywhere you are (1 Corinthians 14:28).

12. When you pray in tongues you give thanks and praises very well (1 Corinthians 14:17).

13. When you pray in tongues it is a sign to the world that Christ is in you (Mark 16:17).

14. When you pray in tongues you have taken the first step into supernatural things (Acts 2:4).

15. When you pray in tongues you are exercising faith (Galatians 3:5).

16. When you pray in tongues you are doing what great men like Paul did (1 Corinthians 14:18; Hebrews 6:12).

17. When you pray in tongues you can pray against your enemies (in their presence) without their knowing what you are saying (1 Corinthians 14:2).

18. When you pray in tongues you can pray and think (1 Corinthians 14:14).

19. When you pray in tongues you can pray and study secular books (1 Corinthians 14:14).

20. When you pray in tongues you can pray and read your Bible (1 Corinthians 14:14).

21. When you pray in tongues you can pray and read other books (1 Corinthians 14:14).

22. When you pray in tongues you can pray and listen to CDs (1 Corinthians 14:14)

23. When you pray in tongues you can pray and watch videos (1 Corinthians 14:14).

24. When you pray in tongues you can pray and still do your work (1 Corinthians 14:14).

25. When you pray in tongues you can walk around and pray (1 Corinthians 14:14).

Chapter 6

The Three Greatest Prayer Topics

Someone may ask, "What do I pray about for one whole hour? I do not have anything to say after five minutes!" I have had that experience many times. Many Christians begin to look at their watches after one and a half minutes of prayer. Somehow, it seems there is nothing left to say. That is why you need prayer topics.

What is a prayer topic? A prayer topic is something that gives you guidelines for prayer. When you read through the Bible, you will discover exactly what to pray about. These are the prayer topics you need. I want to share with you three of the most important groups of prayer topics so you can develop a powerful prayer life.

1. The Topics in the Lord's Prayer

After this manner therefore pray ye: Our Father which art in Heaven, Hallowed be thy name. Thy kingdom come. Thy will be done in earth, as it is in Heaven. Give us this day our daily bread. And forgive us our debts, as we forgive our debtors. And lead us not into temptation, but deliver us from evil: For thine is the kingdom, and the power, and the glory, forever. Amen.

Matthew 6:9-13

One of the things that struck the disciples about the Lord Jesus was His ability to pray for long hours. They wanted to know what strategy, formula or trick He used in order to stay in prayer for such long hours.

55

That is why they approached Him and said, "Lord, teach us how to pray." They needed to have a sort of guideline for their prayer lives. Jesus sat them down and gave them eight steps to enhance their personal prayer lives.

1. Give Thanks and Worship the Lord

...Our Father which art in Heaven, Hallowed be thy name.

Matthew 6:9

Jesus taught us that the first step is to say thank you and to worship the Lord. The first thing to do in this prayer formula is to spend time giving thanks to the Lord. For most people thanksgiving lasts for approximately forty-five seconds.

However, we need to be grateful to the Lord for all that He has done for us. Thank Him for allowing you to see that day. Many people die every day, it could have been you. The fact that you are alive is a miracle. Thank Him for your pastor and your church.

Thank Him that you can read this book. I have members in my Bible school who cannot write. During the classes, they have to record what is said on tape. They simply do not have the ability to read or write. I thank God for the fact that I am in the ministry. The fact that you are reading my book is a miracle of God.

Some people can only see problems. God is touching your eyes right now! He is opening your eyes to see His blessings all around. In this first step of prayer, you must thank the Lord for what He has done for you.

A Sad Visit

I recently visited a friend of mine. He lived virtually on the street. He had become a drug addict, and he had no food or money. As I took some money out of my pocket to give to him, tears welled up in my eyes. I thought of how pathetic this young man's condition was. I realized that it could have been me. Somehow, by the grace of God I had come to know the Lord. I could have been smoking marijuana. After all, I saw many people doing it when I was younger. I could have been dead and buried long ago.

I have been in near-fatal car crashes. I have been in planes that almost collided with other planes on the runway. On two different occasions, I have been in aircrafts that landed and had to do an emergency takeoff in order to avoid a collision on the runway. But I am still here and I know I have something to thank God for.

My friends, if you cannot find something to thank God for you may have an ungrateful spirit.

2. Pray for the Kingdom of God to Come

Thy kingdom come...

Matthew 6:10

The second important step is to pray for the kingdom of God to come. This step is my favourite step. I can spend three hours here. But if you do not have much time, you can spend just ten minutes on this. Please note here that the order is very important. The first thing is to pray for the church and the kingdom. Ask God to bless the church.

When the church is growing, it is an indication that more people are being saved every day. Everybody is developing his personal kingdom. People are developing their financial strength. Most people do not really care about the church. Every Christian must first pray for the church to develop and grow.

Pray for your pastors instead of criticizing them. Men of God are human beings just like you. Pastors make so many mistakes every day. Pray that God will protect His leaders from attacks of all sorts.

3. God's Will Be Done

...Thy will be done in earth, as it is in heaven.

Matthew 6:10

The third step is to pray for the will of God to be done. Anyone who prays that God's will should be done in his life cares for himself. If you love yourself, pray that the will of God be done in your life. I have come to believe that God's will is better than my will or anybody else's will. Nobody knows the future, but God knows what He has in store for you.

Jesus prayed for three hours in the garden of Gethsemane that the will of God be done. After you have prayed this prayer you can relax and allow events to unfold. When Judas and the Pharisees came to arrest Christ, He did not resist them. He believed and accepted that the events that were happening were the will of God, and indeed they were. Those events were leading him to his greatest victory over Satan.

If you want to have peace and confidence in this life, spend time praying that the will of God comes to pass in your life.

Many years ago, I was a young medical student. I had no idea that I would be where I am today. In 1985, during the first term of my third year, I spent many hours praying that the will of God be done. Our school campus was near the Atlantic Ocean. Every night at 10 o'clock I went along with four other friends to the beach. I clearly remember standing on the rocks on the beach and praying, "Oh Lord, let thy will be done."

As I stood on the dark shores of Ghana, I remembered how missionaries came to our nation and sacrificed their lives. I lifted up my hands on the beach and said, "Use me Lord. Let your will be done." I cried to the Lord and said, "You brought me here. I do not know the future. Whatever you want to be done, let it come to pass." I believe that today I am walking in the answers of those prayers. For several weeks, I prayed those same prayers.

Begin to spend time praying to God for His will to be done. Do you think the will of God will happen naturally? Certainly not! If it was going to happen naturally why would you have to spend time praying about it? The very fact that Jesus taught us to pray about it means that it is not automatic that the will of God will happen.

I see your future unfolding in a positive way! I see God lifting you up as you pray about His will! I see you marrying the right person as you spend time praying for the will of God to be done!

4. Our Daily Bread

Give us this day our daily bread.

Matthew 6:11

The next step is to pray for your daily bread. Jesus taught us to pray for our daily needs. That means we are to pray about our jobs, marriages and everything that concerns us.

Some years ago I felt I was too spiritual to marry. But no one can be more spiritual than God. Do not be too spiritual to ask God for your physical needs. Ask Him for a house. Ask Him for bread. Do you want a husband? God is granting him to you right now as you read this book. Pray to the Lord for yourself. Spend some minutes mentioning your needs to the Lord. If you spend another ten minutes asking the Lord for your daily needs, your life will change dramatically.

When it comes to prayer do not depend on anyone, depend on yourself. Do not expect somebody to pray for you. Many times, people who you think are praying for you are actually sleeping.

God is giving you a formula for prayer. Operate in it and walk in your blessings.

5. Pray for Forgiveness

And forgive us our debts, as we forgive our debtors.

Matthew 6:12

The next step is to pray for forgiveness. We all need forgiveness for our sins. There are two types of sins: sins of commission and sins of omission. We must be aware of our sinful nature as we approach the throne of grace.

Appropriate the blood of Jesus for yourself. Ask the Lord to see you only through the eyes of the blood.

One of the first sins of commission is the sin of the mouth: lying, flattery, backbiting, gossip, etc. Another arena for sin is the mind. Many of us have committed murder, adultery and stealing in our minds. Our minds are often polluted with sin. We must come before the Lord and pray for mercy. As we ask the Lord for mercy, we must search our hearts to see whether we have forgiven the people around us.

Sometimes I listen to the way people condemn those who have made mistakes. It makes me sad! Are we not all human? Are we not all subject to the same temptations? Is it not by the grace of God that we survive? When we come to this part of the prayer, we must correct any judgemental or arrogant attitudes.

One of the important sins to confess is the sin of omission. There are people who go to Hell because a neighbour did not witness to them. There are friends who die and go to Hell because we never told them about Christ. As we come before the throne, God sees all our mistakes. If we act as though we are perfect, we deceive ourselves and the truth is not in us. Spend time asking the Lord to have mercy on your life.

6. Pray against Temptation

And lead us not into temptation...

Matthew 6:13

The next important step in The Lord's prayer formula is to pray against temptation. We are all human beings. When I hear of great men of God falling, I become so frightened. I wonder about myself. Many times I just pray that I will just make it safely to Heaven. It is important for you to pray against temptations in your life. You may not know, but prayer strengthens you against temptations.

Fasting Without Prayer Is Dieting

On the night of betrayal, Jesus gave the disciples an eternal command, "Pray in case you fall into a temptation." Many years ago, I remember fasting for three days. By the third day, I was so weak that I could not rise out of the bed. This was the first time I had fasted for three days without any food at all. Because we had not prayed, I was almost unconscious.

Some months later I decided to try this fast again. This time I decided to wake up at 4 a.m. and spend a couple of hours in prayer before the day began. By the third day of the fast, I was still strong. There was a great difference between the two fasts. I had such strength because I had been more prayerful.

My Christian friend, prayer is a supernatural act and provides strength even when your flesh is weak.

7. Pray that God Delivers You from Evil

...deliver us from evil...

Matthew 6:13

The seventh step is to pray that God should deliver you from evil. It is important for you to pray against the evils in this world. Cover yourself with the blood of Jesus. The Israelites would sprinkle the blood of lambs over the lintels and doorposts. This was to prevent any evil from coming into the home. We are to do the same thing now but in a spiritual way.

And they shall take of the blood, and strike it on the two side posts and on the upper door post...AND WHEN I SEE THE BLOOD, I WILL PASS OVER YOU...

Exodus 12:7,13

How do you sprinkle the blood? You sprinkle the blood of Jesus with your words. Apply the blood of Jesus over every part of your home and family. Place an injunction over every flying witch. Declare that your household is a no-fly-zone for every witch, wizard or evil presence. Cancel every enchantment, spell, charm or lamentation that has been taken up against you. Declare that you will live and not die. Bind Satan and his agents. Have faith in God. Command angelic beings and the forces of Heaven to be on guard around you. God will keep you as you pray against evil in your life.

8. Thank Him and Give Him Glory

...For thine is the kingdom, and the power, and the glory, forever. Amen.

Matthew 6:13

The final topic in the Lord's Prayer is to thank Him and to give Him glory. For thine is the kingdom, the power and the glory. Thank Him over and over. Declare that He is more powerful than the walls of opposition in your life. Declare that every mountain of impossibility is possible because of His power and His glory.

Lift up your hands and speak about His glorious power in your life. Declare that every serpentine agenda for your life cannot happen because of the power, kingdom and the glory of God. Thank Jehovah that He has time for you to listen to your prayer. Thank Him that it is well with your soul. Thank Him that it is well with you.

If you follow these steps, you will have at least an hour of effective and fruitful prayer every day.

It is my prayer that these strategies for prayer will revolutionize your spiritual life. May you move into greater heights in God's kingdom, as you apply the principles in this book.

2. The Ephesians Prayer Topics

Many people just gloss over Ephesians chapter one. They think it is too complicated to understand. However, God reveals to us major topics for prayer in this chapter. I call them the Ephesians prayer formula. The Ephesians prayer topics have six important components.

- The 1st step is to give thanks with a grateful heart.
- The 2nd step is to pray for wisdom and revelation in the knowledge of Him.
- The 3rd step is to pray for the eyes of your understanding to be enlightened.
- The 4th step is to pray to know your calling and the hope of your calling.
- The 5th step is to pray to know the riches of the inheritance of the saints.
- The 6th step is to pray to know the power of God.

Wherefore I also, after I heard of your faith in the Lord Jesus, and love unto all the saints, Cease not to give thanks for you, making mention of you in my prayers;

That the God of our Lord Jesus Christ, the Father of glory, may GIVE UNTO YOU THE SPIRIT OF WISDOM AND REVELATION in the knowledge of him:

The EYES OF YOUR UNDERSTANDING BEING ENLIGHTENED; that YE MAY KNOW WHAT IS THE HOPE OF HIS CALLING, and what the riches of the glory of his inheritance in the saints,

And WHAT IS THE EXCEEDING GREATNESS OF HIS POWER TO US-WARD who believe, according to the working of his mighty power, Which he wrought in Christ, when he raised him from the dead, and set him at his own right hand in the heavenly places,

Ephesians 1:15-21

a. Give Thanks

Cease not to GIVE THANKS for you...

Ephesians 1:16

First of all, you must give thanks. Many people have become hardened and ungrateful. It is nice when you meet a few grateful people among the masses of ungrateful people in the world! The first thing to do therefore, under this prayer formula, is to spend quality time thanking the Lord in prayer. Thank Him for His goodness and mercies, thank Him for His protection, thank Him for His provision — the list is endless!

b. Cry to the Lord for Revelation

The second important step is to cry out to the Lord for revelation. This is one of my favourite prayer topics. You may know something, but until it is revealed to you in a deeper way, you do not really know it! There is a difference between "head" knowledge and "revelation" knowledge.

That the God of our Lord Jesus Christ, the Father of glory, may give unto you the SPIRIT OF WISDOM AND REVELATION IN THE KNOWLEDGE OF HIM:
Ephesians 1:17

I have always known that it is dangerous to drive very fast. I have seen large billboards that declare, *"The speed that thrills is the speed that kills."* One day, I travelled to Tamale in the northern region of Ghana. I was driving at over 120 kilometres per hour when suddenly a cyclist crossed my path. I soon found myself somersaulting in the air. After that experience, I had revelation knowledge about driving too fast!

I remember one night I was on a highway driving at about eighty kilometres per hour when suddenly three cars overtook me with the speed of a bullet. Such was their speed that it looked as though my car was stationary. I smiled and thought to myself, "There was a time no car ever overtook me on a highway. These people do not have revelation knowledge." What I had experienced had given me a deeper understanding of the knowledge about driving fast. We call this type of knowledge - revelation knowledge.

There is a difference between knowing something and having a revelation about it. The more I pray for revelation, the more I understand the Word of God. The cardinal thing that has taken me forward in my walk with God has been the revelation I have had in His Word. When you have had a revelation, you change. The cardinal sign of revelation is a change in your life.

Every year I have a deeper and progressive revelation of God and His Word. If you are a pastor, spend hours praying for wisdom and revelation. God anoints people who know Him. When I say know Him, I am talking about having a revelation of God through His Word. The things I am sharing with you in this book are things I know by revelation. They are more real to me than facts from a history book.

Life is short and the only thing worth doing is the work of the ministry. Jesus Himself said to "lay up for yourself treasures in Heaven". The revelation of this Scripture is deep in my heart. But most people do not have a revelation of it. Although many people know this Scripture, it has not been revealed to them. That is why I could give up a lucrative medical career for the ministry. I believe I will one day reap great heavenly rewards that are more valuable than any amount of money.

That is why I could give up a quiet life of wealth and privacy in exchange for a public, often criticized role of a spiritual leader. I have a revelation of the truth, that, "Vanity of vanities...all is vanity" (Ecclesiastes 1:2).

The Lawyer Received Revelation

I once visited a dying man in the hospital. He was a young and successful lawyer struck down in the midst of his years with a deadly disease. I will never forget something he said to me: "If God would raise me up from this bed I will serve Him; even if it means becoming a full-time preacher."

As this man lay dying, he realized how futile everything in this world really was. He suddenly had revelation knowledge about many things that are written in the Bible.

Somehow we read the Bible but we do not get the revelation of it. When you pray for the Spirit of Revelation, things which you have read over and over will come alive to you in a different way.

c. Pray for Understanding

The EYES OF YOUR UNDERSTANDING BEING ENLIGHTENED; that ye may know what is the hope of his calling, and what the riches of the glory of his inheritance in the saints,

Ephesians 1:18

The next step in the Ephesians prayer formula is to pray for understanding. When you have understanding, you know why you should obey the Word of God. I often pray for the Spirit of understanding. When you have understanding, it helps you to obey God's instructions. Because I ask for understanding, God often shows me many deep things in His Word.

That is why I can preach *"Twenty-five Reasons Why We Should Have a Mega Church"*. I once taught, *"One Hundred and Twenty Reasons Why We Should Win Souls"*. Believe it or not, each of those reasons was different. When you have the Spirit of understanding you will know why God is speaking to you the way He is.

There are many Christian wives who are unwilling to do their duties in their marriage. The reason is, they do not have an understanding about the duties of a wife. I notice how the revelation of the importance of the duties of a wife comes alive when tragedy strikes the marriage.

d. Pray about Your Calling

The eyes of your understanding being enlightened; that ye may know what is the HOPE OF HIS CALLING, and

what the riches of the glory of his inheritance in the saints,

Ephesians 1:18

The fourth step in the Ephesians prayer formula is to pray about your calling. Every Christian is called to a ministry.

For we are his workmanship, created in Christ Jesus unto good works, which God hath before ordained that we should walk in them.

Ephesians 2:10

Christians were not recreated for nothing. God intends for every one of us to fulfil our divine call. We are called to do good works. We are called to be unmovable, steadfast, always abounding in the work of the Lord. I watch modern-day Christians attend service after service. Christianity has become a kind of ritual for many people. They just attend church, sing songs and listen to a thirty-minute sermon. But there is more to the calling of God than that. When I became a Christian, I joined a vibrant ministry that went around preaching the Word. To me, Christianity has always been an experience of soul winning and establishing other Christians in the Lord.

The Taxi Driver Did Not Believe Me!

I was once chatting with a taxi driver in London. He asked me where I was coming from. I told him, "I've just flown in from Amsterdam."

He said, "Oh, there are a lot of prostitutes there; did you have a good time?"

I answered, "Oh no! I'm a Christian. We don't live like that!"

He exclaimed, "Are you sure Christians don't do that? Do you really believe that stuff? Do you actually believe in Heaven?"

He went on, "If Heaven is really so nice then why don't you commit suicide and go there right now."

Unfortunately I had got to the end of my journey and could not explain the hope (the reason) of my calling as a Christian. This taxi driver brought up a very valid point. **If we are all just waiting to enter Heaven, why not just go there right away?**

The answer is simple: Christians are not expected to kill themselves! Christians have an important calling to save souls and to establish people in the Lord. We cannot just rush to Heaven now! The hope (reason) for our calling is to bear fruit and win souls in this life. That is why we are still here and have not left for Heaven yet. According to Revelation 14:13, your works will follow you into Heaven.

> **...Blessed are the dead which die in the Lord from henceforth: Yea, saith the Spirit, that they may rest from their labours; and their works do follow them.**
>
> **Revelation 14:13**

What you do on earth will determine how your stay in Heaven will be like. If you know why Christ has saved you, you will have a lot to do for Him here on earth.

e. To Know the Riches of Your Inheritance in Christ

> **The eyes of your understanding being enlightened; that ye may know what is the hope of his calling, and what the RICHES OF THE GLORY OF HIS INHERITANCE IN THE SAINTS,**
>
> **Ephesians 1:18**

The next step is to know the riches of our inheritance in Christ. This means we need to know what we have inherited as Christians.

When my father died, he left properties for his children. A few months after he died, we assembled in Court to listen to the reading of his will. We all wanted to know what the riches of our inheritance were. We took the time to find out what we had inherited. I did not know what my father had given to me. I had to go to the Court to find out for myself. It is sad to say that many Christians do not bother to find out what God has in store for them. When you begin to discover what God has in store for you, you will be amazed. We need to pray to know what God has given to us.

Are We Supposed to Be Poor?

Many people think that Christians are supposed to be poor. They think that pastors, in particular, are supposed to be impoverished. There are people who want ministers to come crawling to their doorsteps to beg for a tin of sardines and a loaf of bread. Is this what we have inherited from our heavenly Father? No, certainly not!

Apostle Peter wanted to find out how he would benefit from following Christ, so he asked:

...Lo, we have left all, and followed thee.

Mark 10:28

In other words, how do we benefit from serving you? Jesus answered him clearly. That answer applies to all of us:

...There is no man that hath left house, or brethren, or sisters, or father, or mother, or wife, or children, or lands, for my sake, and the gospel's, But he shall receive an hundredfold now in this time, houses, and brethren, and sisters, and mothers, and children, and lands, with persecutions; and in the world to come eternal life.

Mark 10:29, 30

The heritage of Christians and ministers is not lack and poverty. But if you do not find out or pray about it you will live in the darkness of that deception all the days of your life.

f. To Know the Greatness of God's Power

And what is the EXCEEDING GREATNESS of his power to us-ward who believe, according to the working of his mighty power,

Ephesians 1:19

The last step of the Ephesians prayer formula is to pray to know the greatness of God's power. There are certain Christians who do not want anything to do with the power of God. In the last days, the Bible teaches that some people will have a form of godliness but will deny the reality of the power of the Gospel (2 Timothy 3:5).

One of the things you need to pray about is to know the power of the Holy Spirit. There are two types of churches in the world: teaching churches and power churches.

Some churches emphasize the teaching of the Word and have nothing to do with the power of God. That is a mistake! You cannot take away miracles from the Bible. Without the miracles of the Bible all we are left with is philosophical literature.

It is because people do not believe in the power of God, that they are frightened by weird looking witches and fetish priests. We need to pray for the power until we experience it. You will not taste of God's power unless you pray for it! Thank God for nice teachings on Sunday. Thank God for good administration. However, there is a power dimension to Christianity and God wants you to experience it too.

3. Timothy's Prayer Topics

Timothy's prayer topics are the next important set of topics. Here it goes:

I exhort therefore, that, first of all, supplications, prayers, intercessions, and giving of thanks, be made for all men; For kings, and for all that are in authority; that we may lead a quiet and peaceable life in all godliness and

honesty. For this is good and acceptable in the sight of God our Saviour;

1 Timothy 2:1-3

This Scripture tells us the types of prayers we must pray, and whom we must pray for. It tells us to pray for all men and specifically for leaders; Heads of State, and anyone who has some form of authority over our lives. This prayer formula does not teach us to curse our leaders or to wish them evil.

There are four types of prayers we are to offer for each person who is in authority: Supplications, prayers, intercessions and giving of thanks. We are to take each leader and pray that God would supply their needs. We are to thank God for their lives. We are to pray generally for them. Finally, we are to intercede for them.

Anyone who uses Timothy's prayer topics will experience four blessings from the Lord. You will experience a quiet life, a peaceful life, a godly life and an honest life. Whoever you are, this prayer formula can apply to you. There is always someone who has some form of authority over your life.

In my country, we have a President and a parliament who rule in the affairs of our nation. One way or the other, the decisions they take affect everyone. Recently, the entire country experienced a major power crisis which led to severe power rationing. Our church activities were greatly affected. Whether we liked it or not, the decisions taken by those in charge of electricity generation were affecting us.

The Word of God says that prayer for our leaders is important if we want to continue living a godly life.

Years ago, I was going to a broadcasting station to do a recording with a Christian group. When I got to a place called Danquah Circle, I realized that there was not a single car or human being in sight even though this was normally a very busy area. When I heard the sound of heavy artillery, I decided to retreat to my home for my dear life's sake. I later found out that there had been a military coup in the city. Some soldiers had decided to overthrow the government of the day. Because of this coup d'état, our Christian recording for television could not take place. Once again, we could not lead our godly lives because of instability in our nation's leadership.

Kings and Princes

There are certain parts of the world which are no-go zones. Missionary work and church work have grounded to a halt because it is not safe to be there. This is why God tells us to pray for kings and people in authority.

If you study Ezekiel, you will find out that although there was a King of Tyrus in the natural, there was also a King of Tyrus in the spirit realm.

...Son of man, say to the leader of Tyre, "Thus says the Lord GOD, Because your heart is lifted up And you have said, 'I am a god, I sit in the seat of gods, In the heart of the seas' ; YET YOU ARE A MAN and not God, Although you make your heart like the heart of God--"
Ezekiel 28:2, (NASB)

Son of man, take up a lamentation over the king of Tyre, and say to him, 'Thus says the Lord GOD, "You had the seal of perfection, Full of wisdom and perfect in beauty.

YOU WERE IN EDEN, the garden of God; Every precious stone was your covering: The ruby, the topaz, and the diamond; The beryl, the onyx, and the jasper; The lapis lazuli, the turquoise, and the emerald; And the gold, the workmanship of your settings and sockets, Was in you. On the day that you were created They were prepared.

YOU WERE THE ANOINTED CHERUB who covers, And I placed you there. You were on the holy mountain of God; You walked in the midst of the stones of fire.
Ezekiel 28:12-14, (NASB)

Tyrus had a supernatural being that ruled its affairs. This fellow was also called the king of Tyrus. Why was he called the king of Tyrus? Because he actually governed and ruled in Tyrus!

When Jesus was tempted in the wilderness, one of the offers that Satan made to Him was to give Him all of the kingdoms of the world. If Satan could not have given the kingdoms of the world to Jesus, it would not have been a temptation. It was a real temptation to Jesus because Satan was actually the one in control of the kingdoms of the world. You cannot give something that you do not have!

You and I can see that the world is headed towards eventual annihilation. There will probably be a nuclear war one-day. Some people sing, *"He's got the whole world in His hands."* I do not believe that is true. If the Lord had the whole world in His hands, the world would not be in the mess that it is in. If Jesus was ruling this world, there would not be wars in Rwanda, Burundi, Angola, Ethiopia, Eritrea, Central African Republic, Liberia, Sierra Leone, Democratic Republic of Congo, Congo Brazzaville, Bosnia, Afghanistan, Israel, Palestine and the list goes on!

If Jesus were in control of this world there would not be such injustice and wickedness throughout the world. The Bible tells us clearly that Satan is the god of this world.

In whom the god of this world hath blinded the minds of them which believe not, lest the light of the glorious gospel of Christ, who is the image of God, should shine unto them.

2 Corinthians 4:4

For some reason, Satan seems to have legal control over the nations of this earth. **Before God can intervene in the affairs of men, He has to be invited by a legitimate citizen of this world.** You and I are legitimate members of the world community. If the Lord gets involved without a legal invitation, Satan can accuse Him of the crime of illegal takeovers, such as happened with Iraq and Kuwait.

God is waiting for our invitation through prayer. When we invite Him to build our nations in freedom, justice and peace, He will do just that. Whenever Christians pray for leaders, there is a change.

Once, Abraham's wife was illegally taken by the king of the day. God appeared to the king called Abimelech, and said, "You are a dead man. You have taken somebody's wife to be your own." The king was scared; he thought he was going to die. But God told him, "Tell Abraham to pray for you."

Now therefore restore the man his wife; for he is a prophet, and he [Abraham] shall pray for thee, and thou shalt live: and if thou restore her not, know thou that thou shalt surely die, thou, and all that are thine.

Genesis 20:7

Why did God not deliver Abimelech right away? After all, He knew about the prayer that Abraham was going to pray. But no, God has to wait for the invitation of men before getting involved in the affairs of this world.

There are three main reasons why we need to pray for those in authority. First, we have to pray that the decisions of the nation will not be based on selfish and political desires only. The second reason is that the nature of all men is to grab and take as much as they can. We have to pray against corruption. Thirdly, we must pray for peace and freedom so that we may go about our Christian duties without any hindrance. We need to pray that our leaders will truly love the nation. How can you know when a leader loves the nation?

For he loveth our nation and hath built us a synagogue.

Luke 7:5

When a leader loves the nation, he will build the nation and not his personal wealth. If you do not pray for those who have authority over you, your life may become frustrated. The Bible tells us that the heart of the king is in the hand of the Lord, and He turns it whichever way he wants.

The king's heart is in the hand of The Lord, as the rivers of water: he turneth it whithersoever he will.

Proverbs 21:1

In Genesis chapter 40, you will find a very interesting story. There was a king who had a butler and a baker. The butler was in charge of everything in the home. The baker made biscuits, cakes and pies that the king enjoyed eating. Something happened in the workplace that made the king angry with both the butler and the baker. In his wrath, he had them thrown into prison. Whilst there, each of them had a dream which Joseph (who had been wrongfully imprisoned) interpreted. He predicted that the butler would be re-instated and the baker would lose his life.

Now, understand that both the butler and the baker were in trouble. Their very lives depended on the one they had displeased. Everything depended on how Pharaoh thought. Depending on his decision, someone would live or die. In this particular case, the baker died, just as Joseph predicted. **There are times when your life depends on what someone thinks about you!**

The more you pray Timothy's prayer, the more favourable the thoughts of your boss will be towards you. I see you having favour in all that you do! I see the heart of the king having mercy on you!

Many young people must pray for their fathers in order to have the favour of God. I remember when I was in the university, I asked my father for a car. I realized that my father was spending a lot of money on horse racing. You see, my father had one of the largest horse racing stables in the country. He employed many people and bought horses from all over West Africa. I thought to myself, "If my father wants to, he can buy a brand new car for me."

One day, my father decided to buy a car for me. My prayers for him made the Lord turn his heart in my favour. I received a brand new car when I was in fifth year medical school. I rejoiced and used that car for the glory of God. I was the first church member of Lighthouse Chapel International to own a car. My car became the church bus and the church taxi. And I was happy to do it, because I knew that the Lord had provided. God can bless you through those who are in authority over you.

As you pray for them, God will give you favour! Things are changing in your favour! I see God turning the heart of every king in your life! They will decide not to kill you anymore. They will decide that you must live! I see many blessings rising up to embrace you! **As you pray for fathers, bosses and presidents, you will experience only godliness, peace and quietness.**

From today, every wife that prays for her husband will experience quietness in her house! From now on, your "unbeliever" husband will allow you to go to church! He will not stop you from going for all-night prayer meetings! He will not oppose your Christian life anymore because you are praying for him!

Chapter 7

How to Pray With All Kinds of Prayer

Praying always with all [kinds of] prayer and supplication in the Spirit, and watching thereunto with all perseverance and supplication for all saints;
Ephesians 6:18

There are different kinds of prayer; different strokes for different folks, as they say. There are different types of prayers that must be used for different types of situations. In this life, you will experience a wide variety of situations. Thankfully, God has provided us with a wide variety of prayer types. Let us consider a few of these.

Eight Different Kinds of Prayers

1. The Prayer of Consecration

In this type of prayer you offer yourself to the Lord for His perfect will to be done. God loves His children who want His will to be done.

If you pray this prayer of consecration, God will be more likely to listen to your other prayers. Some people know only "give me, give me, give me" prayers. There are times God is not interested in answering such prayers. He wants to hear a prayer of consecration.

Learn to spend hours asking the Lord for His will to be done. Jesus prayed in the garden of Gethsemane for three hours. He had only one prayer topic. He did not pray about seventeen different things.

...and prayed, saying, O my Father, if it be possible, let this cup pass from me: nevertheless, not as I will, but as thou wilt.

Matthew 26:39

Every Christian must have the prayer of consecration as one of his prayer topics. Pray that God will perform His will in your life. This prayer topic puts all other prayer topics in their right perspective. That is why I mentioned it as the first type of prayer that you need to pray.

2. Praying in the Spirit

But ye, beloved, building up yourselves on your most holy faith, praying in the Holy Ghost

Jude 20

What is praying in the Spirit? The answer is in the Bible.

For he that speaketh in an unknown tongue speaketh not unto men, but unto God: for no man understandeth him; howbeit in the spirit he speaketh mysteries.

1 Corinthians 14:2

Every Christian can speak to God in mysteries. Praying in tongues is praying in the Spirit. God wants you to pray in tongues. A large percentage of my prayer is prayer "in the Spirit". I can give you many reasons why you should pray in tongues. One reason is that when you pray in the Spirit, God directs your prayer Himself. He leads you to ask Him for what is necessary. In Acts 2, the Bible says that the Spirit gave them utterance when they spoke in tongues. When the Spirit gives you utterance, it means the Spirit is giving you the words to say. What better deal could you have?

Another important reason why you should pray in the Spirit is that it builds you up. 1 Corinthians 14:4 tells us that he who speaks in an unknown tongue edifies himself. The word *edify* speaks of charging up yourself in the way a car battery is charged. We all need that regular spiritual charge up.

3. The Prayer of Faith

And the prayer of faith shall save the sick...

James 5:15

The prayer of faith is a prayer which has a great expression of faith. In Mark 11:24, the Bible teaches us to believe that we have already received what we prayed for. Believing that you have already received is different from believing that you will receive it one day.

Prayers of faith are especially effective against sickness and disease. As I said earlier, different types of prayer can be used to solve different problems.

4. The Prayer of Confession of Sins

It is important for us to confess our sins on a regular basis. Prayer which does not include prayer for forgiveness is insufficient. We must always ask for mercy. We must pray for it! If we say that we are perfect, we are foolishly deceived.

If we say that we have no sin, we deceive ourselves, and the truth is not in us.

1 John 1:8

5. The Short and Powerful Prayer

And when they had sent away the multitude, they took him even as he was in the ship. And there were also with him other little ships. And there arose a great storm of wind, and the waves beat into the ship, so that it was now full. And he was in the hinder part of the ship, asleep on a pillow: and they awake him and say unto him, Master, carest thou not that we perish? And he arose, and rebuked the wind, and said unto the sea, Peace, be still. And the wind ceased, and there was a great calm.

Mark 4:36-39

In this Scripture, Jesus found Himself in a crisis situation. He and His disciples were caught up in the middle of a very dangerous storm, and their very lives were being threatened. There was no time to find a quiet place to pray for the hand of God to move on their behalf. He just prayed a short but powerful prayer and the storm ceased!

Also in John 11:41,42, Jesus encountered another situation that demanded an immediate response. He needed a miracle for his family friends. His old pal Lazarus had been dead for four days. Everyone was looking up to him. Could he go away and pray for three hours? The answer is no!

He had to pray a short prayer and He needed results immediately. Listen to His prayer:

> **…And Jesus lifted up his eyes, and said, Father, I thank thee that thou hast heard me. And I knew that thou hearest me always: but because of the people which stand by I said it, that they may believe that thou hast sent me.**
>
> **John 11:41,42**

These types of prayers come in handy when you are faced with a crisis situation. There is no time to retreat and pray. Pray a short and powerful prayer when you need to and believe that God has heard you. After the short and powerful prayer, act boldly just like Jesus did! You will have one hundred per cent results.

6. The Long Prayer

There are times that it is important to spend a long time in prayer. Jesus did this very often.

> **And it came to pass in those days, that he went out into a mountain to pray, and continued all night in prayer to God.**
>
> **Luke 6:12**

And in the morning, rising up a great while before day, he went out and departed into a solitary place, and there prayed.

Mark 1:35

You will notice that in both cases Jesus spent long hours praying. A great while is a long time. All night is also a long time. Develop the art of praying for several hours. Start with one hour and graduate to three hours. Then progress to five and seven hours!

Learn to pray all day and all night long. You will experience one hundred per cent answers to your prayers. There are times you need to spend many hours in prayer.

If Jesus had to pray for long hours, then you will also have to. There are times you do not have to change the prayer topic. You can pray on the same topic for hours. Jesus did it! It is not useless repetition, it is praying like Jesus did.

7. Loud Prayers

Who in the days of his flesh, when he had offered up prayers and supplications with strong crying and tears unto him that was able to save him from death, and was heard that in he feared;

Hebrews 5:7

Jesus prayed with strong cries and so can you. There is a difference between meditation and prayer. Some people claim to pray in their minds. What is the difference between praying in your mind and meditation? I think there is no difference! I am not saying that you must always shout when you pray. Ninety per cent of the time you cannot hear me when I am praying. I usually pray very quietly. But there are times I pray with strong cries and tears. It is a dimension you must get into. There are some things that will only happen in your life when you pray like Jesus did.

8. Prayer of Thanksgiving

In every thing give thanks: for this is the will of God in Christ Jesus concerning you.

1 Thessalonians 5:18

God wants us to give thanks. Apart from the usual "give me, give me, give me" prayers, God would love to hear some other types of prayers. He would love to hear you say "thank you". Discover the power of thanking the Lord. As you thank Him you will experience many breakthroughs.

Paul and Silas were in jail but they prayed and sang praises at midnight. They gave thanks to God at midnight. Suddenly, there was an earthquake and their chains were broken. This is the power of the prayer of thanksgiving. Even in the midnight of your life, a prayer of thanksgiving is appropriate. There are times in which it will be the most powerful type of prayer you can offer. It is the prayer that leads to earthquakes and broken bands. Move into this type of prayer and experience God's breakthrough for your life.

There is no darkness that can keep you down. There is no "midnight" that can keep you bound when you learn how to give thanks.

It is my prayer that your prayer life will rise into the realm of answered prayer. God is your Father in Heaven. He has to answer your prayers. In fact, He loves to answer your prayers! This is your hour for answers to all your prayers. Indeed, there shall be a performance of all that God has said.

Chapter 8

Does God Answer All
Our Prayers?

There are some verses in the Bible that give the impression that God answers all prayers. But it is obvious that God does not answer all prayers. It is important to look at the broad context of the Bible to understand if and how God answers prayer. The following verses give the impression that God does answer every single prayer.

Perhaps the greatest lesson we can learn from these Scriptures is that God does want to answer 100 per cent of our prayers. That must be our aim. We must aim for God's best – to have 100 per cent of our prayers answered. But there are conditions for answered prayer and in the next chapter, we will consider twelve very important conditions for you to get answers to all your prayers. Notice these Scriptures which strongly promise answers to our prayers.

And all things, whatsoever ye shall ask in prayer, believing, ye shall receive.

Matthew 21:22

And whatsoever ye shall ask in my name, that will I do, that the Father may be glorified in the Son. If ye shall ask any thing in my name, I will do it.

John 14:13-14

Ye have not chosen me, but I have chosen you, and ordained you, that ye should go and bring forth fruit, and that your fruit should remain: that whatsoever ye shall ask of the Father in my name, he may give it you.

John 15:16

And in that day ye shall ask me nothing. Verily, verily, I say unto you, Whatsoever ye shall ask the Father in my name, he will give it you.

Hitherto have ye asked nothing in my name: ask, and ye shall receive, that your joy may be full.

John 16:23-24

For verily I say unto you, That whosoever shall say unto this mountain, Be thou removed, and be thou cast into the sea; and shall not doubt in his heart, but shall believe that those things which he saith shall come to pass; he shall have whatsoever he saith.

Therefore I say unto you, What things soever ye desire, when ye pray, believe that ye receive them, and ye shall have them.

Mark 11:23-24

Chapter 9

Twelve Steps to 100 Per Cent Answered Prayer

P rayer is a privilege that God has given to His children. We can talk to our heavenly Father directly and receive answers. I realize from the attitudes of many Christians that they do not believe that God really answers prayer. But why pray if you will not get results? I believe that you can have one hundred per cent results every time you pray.

Why pray if you will not receive an answer?

Many people take prayer to be some kind of religious routine they must perform. God's Word guarantees us a hundred per cent results every time we pray.

If you look closely at the Scriptures that speak about prayer, you will discover that Jesus did not say that we might possibly (perhaps, maybe, in the sweet by and by, all things being equal) get an answer to our prayers. He said that we *would* get an answer!

I wrote this book for you! I want you to receive one hundred per cent results every time you pray. If it is real, it is real! If it is not real, it is not real! If God exists, then He *can* answer your prayer.

Is God alive? Is He real? Can He hear? Is He deaf? I am sure you know the answers to these questions. God is alive and well and He wants to bless you.

If my God were a piece of wood or a stone, I would not serve Him. We do not worship the sun, the moon or the rivers. We worship a Living God who has power to save and to deliver.

Elijah once challenged the false prophets of Baal. He told them, "There is no use in serving a god who is not available. Our God is either alive or He is dead."

...Elijah mocked them, and said, Cry aloud: for he is a god; either he is talking or he is pursuing [using the bathroom!], or he is in a journey, or peradventure he sleepeth, and must be awaked.

1 Kings 18:27

The god Did Not Speak!

Some years ago, a friend of mine went to a city about a hundred kilometres outside of Accra, the capital city of Ghana. He was accompanying his parents to their hometown. Whilst in the town he had the urge to urinate. Unfortunately, there was no appropriate toilet around so he went into an open space to relieve himself. As he was urinating, he heard screams and shouts from behind. Since he was already in the process, he had to finish. Then he turned round to face the anger of some local residents.

"What are you doing?" they exclaimed. "How can you do this?"

They went on, "You are urinating on our *god*!! Don't you know that the stone on which you are urinating is our *god*?"

This young man apologized profusely but there was nothing he could do about it. He had already bathed their god in his urine!

When I heard this story I thought to myself, "If you are a god, can you not say anything when people urinate on you? Can you not protest at the first sprinkle of urine? If you are a god, at least say something when someone urinates on you!"

What am I trying to say? If God is alive, then He must be able to respond to you. He has given us His Word and He has promised to answer our prayers every time.

He shall call upon me, and I will answer him.

Psalm 91:15

Then shalt thou call, and the Lord shall answer...

Isaiah 58:9

These Scriptures tell us that God *will* answer us. God *shall* answer! How much more definite can it be? Either the Bible is true or it is not true. Either you believe it or you do not! Jesus said,

And I say unto you, Ask, and it *shall* be given you; seek, and ye *shall* find; knock, and it *shall* be opened unto you.

Luke 11:9

There is no word that expresses a stronger assertion than the word shall. I see God answering your prayers right now! By the time you finish reading this chapter, you will experience 100 per cent answers to all your prayers.

1.   ***THE FIRST STEP TO ONE HUNDRED PER CENT ANSWERED PRAYER IS: LEARN HOW TO PRAY YOURSELF WITHOUT NEEDING ANYONE ELSE TO PRAY FOR YOU.***

Jesus taught us to pray to our heavenly Father. Many people do not know how to pray for themselves. They want somebody else to pray for them. They ask the pastor to pray for them. They kneel down before prophets and request special prayers. *There is nothing wrong with being prayed for. But God wants you to learn how to pray for yourself!*

There are some pastors who entrust themselves to prayer warriors. They depend on other people to pray for them. But you must consider the prayer support of friends and prayer warriors as an extra bonus. If it happens – fine! If it does not happen – fine! You cannot depend on it.

Your Christian life should not depend on another person's prayers.

Jesus said, "*You* ask the Father." *You* are supposed to be able to pray yourself.

Remember that the prayers of a righteous man avail much (James 5:16). You are the righteousness of God in Christ (2 Corinthians 5:21). You are righteous! You are righteous enough to get results for your prayers!

Start praying for yourself now! Do not depend only on your pastor. He may be snoring when you think he is praying for you!

2. THE SECOND STEP TO ONE HUNDRED PER CENT ANSWERED PRAYER IS: PRAY TO YOUR HEAVENLY FATHER AND NOT TO ANYONE ELSE.

And in that day ye shall ask me nothing...

John 16:23

Jesus said that in that day we will not ask *Him* for anything. What day is *that* day? Jesus was talking about the period when He would no longer be with the disciples. Jesus was directing us to pray to the heavenly Father Himself. Is there any difference between praying to Jesus and praying to the heavenly Father? There must be, otherwise Jesus would not have told us what He did!

If you want one hundred per cent results, do what Jesus said you should do. Begin your prayer by saying, "Our Father," "Heavenly Father," "Dear Father," or "Father which art in Heaven," etc. You will begin to experience better results.

Do Not Pray to a Handmaid

Some people pray to Mary. I used to attend a church that prayed to Mary. In fact, I myself prayed to Mary almost every day. I think that our holy mother Mary must be wondering why people are praying to her. I am sure she asks herself, *"What can I do for these people? I am a mere mortal like any one of them."*

Mary herself said that she was a mere servant of the Lord.

And Mary said, Behold the handmaid of the Lord; be it unto me according to thy word.

Luke 1:38

Why would you pray to a handmaid? Jesus did not teach us to pray to His mother. He taught us to pray to His Father. There is a big difference! I can understand how our holy mother Mary is respected for the role she played in bringing Jesus to this world. **She was a great woman and a very special vessel. I truly respect and admire her.** But I cannot pray to her.

I do not believe that she can do anything for me now. I will pray to my heavenly Father and I will receive a hundred per cent results, in the name of Jesus.

3. *THE THIRD STEP TO ONE HUNDRED PER CENT ANSWERED PRAYER IS: PRAY IN THE NAME OF JESUS.*

Unfortunately, many people use the name of Jesus as an exclamation or a swear word. This has caused Christians to lose respect for the power in the name of Jesus. I announce to you that there is power in the name of Jesus! Your heavenly Father will respond when He hears the name of Jesus.

...Verily, verily, I say unto you, Whatsoever ye shall ask the Father in my name he will give it you.

John 16:23

In my church, there are people who try to use my name to get certain things done. They know that the mention of my name in our set-up will lead to rapid results. I have often heard it said, "Bishop said, 'so and so'." Why do people engage in name-dropping? It is because names have power.

The use of a name leads to rapid results. At the name of Jesus, every knee shall bow. Demons respond to the name of Jesus. Sickness responds to the name of Jesus. Satan will bow to the name of Jesus. There is power in that name. In the book of Acts, we see how the name of Jesus healed a man.

Be it known unto you all, and to all the people of Israel, that by the name of Jesus...doth this man stand here before you whole.

Acts 4:10

But it is not only bad things which respond to the name of Jesus. Our heavenly Father Himself responds to the name of Jesus. Jesus told us to use the "name of Jesus" to get responses from the Father. Jesus told us to use His name to get results in prayer. From today, whenever you pray, use the name of Jesus; not only as a ritual, but as a vital key to receiving your blessings from Heaven.

4. *THE FOURTH STEP TO ONE HUNDRED PER CENT ANSWERED PRAYER IS: CONFESS YOUR SINS.*

If we say that we have no sin, we deceive ourselves, and the truth is not in us.

1 John 1:8

To approach God without the consciousness of your sin is a mistake. A very important Scripture to remember is found in Isaiah.

Behold, the LORD'S hand is not shortened, that it cannot save; neither his ear heavy, that it cannot hear:But your iniquities have separated between you and your God, and your sins have hid his face from you, that he will not hear.

Isaiah 59:1-2

God is cut off from our lives because of sin. One of the first things you must do when you pray is to confess your sins: both the ones you know and the ones you are not conscious of. Do not let your iniquities separate you from God. God can reach you when the blood of Jesus has cleansed you.

5. *THE FIFTH STEP TO ONE HUNDRED PER CENT ANSWERED PRAYER IS: ABIDE IN CHRIST.*

If ye abide in me and my words abide in you, ye shall ask what ye will, and it shall be done unto you.

John 15:7

Abiding in Christ is an important key to receiving any type of response from the Lord. If you do not stay in the house, do not expect God to answer any of your prayers. A hundred per cent answered prayer is for people who stay in Christ and in His church. When you wander away from God, you become like the prodigal son. You are far from your Father. The prodigal son did not stay in the house.

He moved out and lived in a far country. He fellowshipped with harlots and ate with pigs. The only help he could get was from pigs! So he "asked the pigs" for some of their food. The pigs had compassion on the prodigal son and they gave him some of their food. Even if his father had wanted to give him food, there was no way he could have. He was simply out of the reach of his father. The prodigal son ended up in the custody of a man who put him to work with swine.

When you do not stay in the house, you will end up with the pigs. Perhaps as you read this book, you realize that being far from God has not helped you. It is time to come back home. Staying in fellowship is an important key to receiving the blessings of the Lord.

But if we walk in the light, as he is in the light, we have fellowship one with another...

1 John 1:7

There are some people who think they can be good Christians without going to church. You are deceiving yourself! If you are walking in the light, you will have fellowship with others who are in the light. That is what this Scripture is telling you.

Are you in the darkness or in the light? If you are in the light you will go to church and fellowship with other Christians.

6. **THE SIXTH STEP TO ONE HUNDRED PER CENT ANSWERED PRAYER IS: LET THE WORD OF GOD ABIDE IN YOU.**

It is important for God's Word to be in you. God does not do anything outside His Word. God's Word will direct you in your relationship with Him. God's Word directs you in prayer. God does not answer foolish prayers; neither does He do things against His Word.

If you want to get one hundred per cent answers to your prayers, stay in the Word.

Order my steps in thy word: and let not any iniquity have dominion over me.

Psalm 119:133

7. **THE SEVENTH STEP TO ONE HUNDRED PER CENT ANSWERED PRAYER IS: OBEY THE COMMAND-MENTS OF THE LORD.**

And whatsoever we ask, we receive of him, because we keep his commandments, and do those things that are pleasing in his sight.

1 John 3:22

This Scripture is very clear. God answers the prayers of people who obey Him. If you are living a life of disobedience, God will not honour your prayers. If you had a disobedient son who did not please you, would you just give him anything he asked for? Certainly not! Neither does your heavenly Father answer the prayers of disobedient children. If God has called you to the ministry, just obey! Your obedience opens the door for answers to your prayers.

It is clear that God answers the prayers of righteous people. Become a righteous man and God will answer your prayers.

Confess your faults one to another, and pray one for another, that ye may be healed. THE effectual fervent PRAYER OF A RIGHTEOUS MAN AVAILETH MUCH.

James 5:16

8. THE EIGHTH STEP TO ONE HUNDRED PER CENT ANSWERED PRAYER IS: BE A FRUIT-BEARING CHRISTIAN.

Ye have not chosen me but I have chosen you, and ordained you, that ye should go and bring forth fruit, and that your fruit should remain: that whatsoever ye shall ask of the Father in my name, he may give it you.

John 15:16

God has linked answered prayer to fruit bearing. This Scripture proves that answered prayer is directly connected to the fruits that a person has.

If you are a born-again Christian, the only reason why you are being kept alive is so that you can bear fruit. After all, Heaven is guaranteed.

You have a place in Heaven after you are born again. What else do you need? Earthly treasures are transient and useless. We are being kept alive on this earth so that we can win souls for Him. God wants every Christian to bear fruit.

One thing that many Christians do not know is that God has linked bearing fruit to answering prayer. The Scripture above is very clear!

God will be happy to answer the prayer of someone who bears fruit. What do you do for God? What fruit are you bearing? If you sit in spiritual barrenness just wanting God to answer prayers, you may wait forever. Some people just know how to say, "Give me!

Give me! Give me!" But what are you contributing to God's kingdom?

There is a link between answered prayer and bearing fruit. Receive this revelation into your spirit and begin to bear fruit from today. Do something in your church. Do not just sit there and watch. Stop being an observer. There is no blessing in being a spectator or a commentator. The blessings of one hundred per cent answered prayer are for Christians who bear fruit.

9. THE NINTH STEP TO ONE HUNDRED PER CENT ANSWERED PRAYER IS: HAVE FAITH EVERY TIME YOU PRAY.

Therefore I say unto you, What things soever ye desire, when ye pray, believe that ye receive them, and ye shall have them.

Mark 11:24

Jesus taught great lessons on faith throughout His ministry. He often emphasized that people were getting blessed because they were using faith.

Now the just shall live by faith: but if any man draw back, my soul shall have no pleasure in him.

Hebrews 10:38

God is saying that if you draw away from faith, He will not be pleased with you. There are those who think that faith is not so important. They tend to draw away from the faith message and faith people. They feel that there must rather be an emphasis on patience, gentleness, holiness and on the other qualities of the fruit of the Spirit.

I strongly believe that these qualities are important and play a special role in the Christian life. However, the importance of the fruit of the Spirit to the Christian experience should not make us play down on the importance of something like faith. The fact that the heart is important does not make the kidneys any less important. Both are necessary, and have special, unique roles to play.

Faith is a very special virtue which has a role in every Christian's life. The Bible says that without faith it is *impossible* to please God.

> **But without faith it is impossible to please him: for he that cometh to God must believe that he is, and that he is a rewarder of them that diligently seek him.**
>
> **Hebrews 11:6**

It is interesting to note that the Word of God does not say: "Without love it is impossible to please God." The Bible does not say: "Without peace it is impossible to please God." The Bible is very clear on this fact: WITHOUT FAITH IT IS *IMPOSSIBLE* TO PLEASE GOD!

Abraham's faith in God was considered to be an act of righteousness. Abraham believed that El' Shaddai was able to give him a child at an old age. Abraham had his faults. He lied about his wife and surrendered her twice to unbeliever kings for their pleasure. In spite of his lying and cowardly behaviour, God was very pleased with Abraham because he had faith.

Maybe by your standards, Abraham would have been disqualified. But he was a great man in God's sight. His greatness was a result of his faith.

> **And being fully persuaded that, what he had promised, he was able also to perform. And therefore IT WAS IMPUTED TO HIM FOR RIGHTEOUSNESS.**
>
> **Romans 4:21,22**

God is happy, impressed and pleased when you believe in Him. When you believe that God will heal you, you make Him happy. When you believe that God will prosper you, you make Him excited. When you believe that your breakthrough is on the way, God is so pleased with you. When you have faith that you will live long, God is provoked to extend your life. When you believe that

God will give you increase and abundance, you excite the deep parts of El' Shaddai. You make Him pour out the milk of His blessings into your life.

From today, never doubt any part of God's Word. Accept that you are the champion He is speaking about. Flow with the message of prosperity, healing and abundance. Always remember that God is happy when you believe in Him.

God is not a God of poverty. Since I came to know the Lord I have not decreased. I do not read about decrease, failure, setbacks and limitations in the Bible. I see only abundance, promotion and deliverance from my enemies. I see God lifting me up every day! God did not bring you to Christ in order to demote and disgrace you. He brought you to Christ to lift and establish you in an abundant life. Jesus came that we might have life and have it more abundantly (John 10:10).

Jesus Blessed the Faith People

Under the ministry of Jesus, several people experienced personal breakthroughs. Who were they? And why did they receive these miracles?

You will remember what Jesus said about the woman with the issue of blood. What was the secret of her breakthrough? Jesus gave the answer in Mark 5:34:

...Daughter, thy faith hath made thee whole...

Mark 5:34

Blind Bartimaeus received his sight miraculously. He was a noisy fellow who disturbed the service. But Jesus took notice of him and healed him.

What was his secret? His secret was faith in God!

...thy faith hath made thee whole...

Mark 10:52

The sinful woman who poured an alabaster box of ointment on Jesus' feet also received a miracle of forgiveness. Jesus said to the woman:

...Thy faith hath saved thee; go in peace.

Luke 7:50

Remember the ten lepers who were healed with only one coming back to say thank you. Jesus said these same words to him:

...Arise, go thy way: thy faith hath made thee whole.

Luke 17:19

Two blind men came to Jesus and asked for the mercy of God. Jesus touched them and healed them. What did He say to them?

...According to your faith be it unto you.

Matthew 9:29

Have you noticed that Jesus never said, "Thy love hath made thee whole."

Jesus never said, "Thy holiness hath saved you."

He never said, "According to your patience, be it unto you."

Why did Jesus not say, "Thy good character hath made thee whole"?

Please do not misunderstand me! I am not saying that these things are not important! I am saying that it is the people's faith that impressed Jesus.

Jesus pointed out over and over that it was their *faith* that had brought the breakthrough. That is why the Bible says that without faith it is impossible to please God.

Have you ever thought of those men who broke through the roof of somebody's house in order to bring their paralyzed friend to Christ? Perhaps they were experienced thieves who were used to breaking into people's homes. Perhaps they were men who were used to jumping the queue and cheating others. But the Bible tells us that Jesus noticed their faith and immediately responded to their needs.

And WHEN HE SAW THEIR FAITH he said unto him, Man, thy sins are forgiven thee.

Luke 5:20

Jesus did not dwell on the wrong they did by jumping the queue or removing the tiles from somebody's roof. **He saw their faith.** Jesus sees your faith. God sees your faith. It is time for you to rise up and believe things in the Word of God. According to your faith, it shall be done unto you!

When you exercise faith in prayer, God responds in the same way that Jesus responded to these men. **He is so impressed with your prayer.** When you believe that you have received, you please God! In order to exercise faith, you must believe that you have received what you are praying for. This means you will not have to pray over and over for the same thing.

Begging and crying is not the same as praying with faith. Many Christians just cry and cry in a spirit of hopelessness. God is not against crying. But He is against faithless weeping. Trust God, He wants to give you the desires of your heart.

Receive answers to your prayers at this very moment, in Jesus name! From today, you must believe that you have received what you are asking for.

10.   *THE TENTH STEP TO ONE HUNDRED PER CENT ANSWERED PRAYER IS: PERSISTENCE.*

Persisting in prayer is a guaranteed way to get one hundred per cent prayer results. Jesus gave two vivid examples of how persistence gives one hundred per cent answered prayer. I want you to read them carefully.

And he said unto them, Which of you shall have a friend, and shall go unto him at midnight, and say unto him, Friend, lend me three loaves;

For a friend of mine in his journey is come to me, and I have nothing to set before him?

And he from within shall answer and say, Trouble me not: the door is now shut, and my children are with me in bed; I cannot rise and give thee.

I say unto you, Though he will not rise and give him, because he is his friend, yet BECAUSE OF HIS IMPORTUNITY he will rise and give him as many as he needeth.

Luke 11:5-8

And he spake a parable unto them to this end, that men ought always to pray, and not to faint;

Saying, There was in a city a judge, which feared not God, neither regarded man:

And there was a widow in that city; and she came unto him, saying, Avenge me of mine adversary.

And he would not for a while: but afterward he said within himself, Though I fear not God, nor regard man;

Yet BECAUSE THIS WIDOW TROUBLETH ME, I will avenge her, LEST BY HER CONTINUAL COMING SHE WEARY ME.

And the Lord said, Hear what the unjust judge saith. And shall not God avenge his own elect, which cry day and night unto him, though he bear long with them?

I tell you that he will avenge them speedily. Nevertheless when the Son of man cometh, shall he find faith on the earth?

Luke 18:1-8

Persisting means repeating! It means you will tirelessly go to the Lord in prayer. It means you will shamelessly cry to the Lord until He responds. Persistence brings results even in the natural. Sometimes I receive a phone call, but I am unable to answer because I am too far from the phone. As I approach the phone, I have often thought to myself, "If only this caller would persist, I will answer the phone." Sometimes by the time I get to the phone, the person has given up. There are some who call back. There are some who keep calling until I answer.

This principle of persistence brings results in many spheres of life. The principle of persistence works in prayer as well. I did not say it, *Jesus* did!

Jesus said very clearly that you would get results if you pray and pray and pray! The reason why you will get results is because you keep praying.

Someone may ask, "Does the principle of persistence not contradict the principle of faith? After all, when using the key of faith you wouldn't have to pray more than once!" What you must understand here is that there are different ways of expressing faith.

Praying once is one expression of faith.

Praying over and over about the same issue, with a determination never to stop until you get an answer is also another expression of faith. Each of these two expressions of faith is valid. Each of these two expressions of faith brings results. Each of these two expressions of faith was recommended by Jesus. Each of these two expressions of faith can make God answer your prayer.

There are many Christians who can testify about how they prayed persistently until God answered! There are also many others who have great testimonies about praying once and receiving answers. Jesus did not teach on only one of these styles of prayer. **He taught both methods and guaranteed one hundred per cent results in each case.**

You can liken faith and persistence to killing a cat in different ways. You can beat it, drown it, poison it, shoot it or decapitate it. All of these methods will lead to a hundred per cent result – a hundred per cent dead cat! Decide today to use any of these two keys. Both of these keys are failure proof. "Faith" prayers work all the time. Persistence works all the time. God has given you two assured methods for receiving 100 per cent answered prayer.

11. *THE ELEVENTH STEP TO ONE HUNDRED PER CENT ANSWERED PRAYER IS: DO NOT PRAY AMISS.*

Ye ask, and receive not, because ye ask amiss...

James 4:3

Unfortunately, many Christians ask God for things He cannot give them. God does not answer prayers that have gone amiss. Praying amiss means that you pray unacceptable, unsuitable, inappropriate, inadmissible, impermissible, unsatisfactory and impossible prayers. God will not do things which are against His principles.

Faith is very different from foolishness. There are many Christians who exhibit silliness when they pray. God is not a fool. Please do not try to make Him one.

The fact that you are allowed to exercise faith does not mean that you should be irrational. When God takes no notice of foolish prayers, do not say that prayer does not work. It is your foolish prayers that are not working.

If you ask God for somebody's husband, you are praying a foolish prayer. Some young men, starting out in life, ask the Lord for huge mansions and fantastically expensive cars. It is true that God wants to bless you, but do not expect God to promote you overnight. Look at your Bible carefully. All the people who were blessed experienced it over a period of several years. If you are a married person and you do not use contraceptives, please do not bind the babies in your wife's womb. God does not respond to foolishness.

If you have a job to do and you do not do it, do not pray that your boss will fall sick.

As you grow older do not bother to pray for your youth to return. It is gone forever. You cannot retrace your steps. There is a natural aging process that you cannot bind or revoke!

Why do you bother to ask God to give you an airplane when you don't even own a bicycle? You might as well ask Him to make you the Queen of England.

If you are praying to God to help you to divorce, you are praying amiss. God does not want you to divorce. How can He help you to divorce?

What therefore God hath joined together, let not man put asunder.

Mark 10:9

God cannot answer when you pray amiss! You may divorce by your own choice, but do not pray amiss. God does not break up marriages, He brings people together.

You must realize that there are divine laws operating in the universe. There is no use praying about things which cannot be done scripturally. I am not talking about the laws of your country. I am talking about the laws of God.

There is no man on this earth who can escape the curse declared over Adam.

IN THE SWEAT OF THY FACE SHALT THOU EAT BREAD till thou return unto the ground; for out of it was thou taken: for dust thou art, and UNTO DUST SHALL THOU RETURN.

Genesis 3:19

All men are experiencing the sweat of this life. All men are returning to dust. All men will go to the grave one day. It is just a matter of time.

No matter who they are, all men have to sweat to prosper. No matter how rich they are they will return to the ground. There is no use praying against it. You cannot pray that you will prosper without working hard. You cannot pray that you will not die. That is illegal! Until Jesus returns, you and I have to go the way of all men. Great men like David knew that there was no escape from death.

Now the days of David drew nigh that he should die; and he charged Solomon his son, saying, I GO THE WAY OF ALL THE EARTH...

I Kings 2:1, 2

What is the way of all the earth? It is the inescapable experience of death that all human beings must go through. There is no use in binding or cancelling it!

You will keep getting disappointed in God. Do not pray that you will not have to work hard. Working hard and sweating your way to prosperity is the legal way for us all to prosper. What you must rather do is to pray for wisdom to alleviate the effects of these curses.

It is the wisdom of medical science that alleviates the trauma of childbirth. Through the wisdom of medical science, many women have experienced little pain in childbirth. Many women have had less sorrow in childbirth through the use of wisdom.

It is the wisdom that comes through education that lightens the load on the sons of Adam. All the sons of Adam will labour, but some labour is easier than others. I would prefer to be a doctor than a cleaner. In both cases, I would go through the sweating process to eat bread. But I assure you that the labour of a doctor is different from that of a cleaner.

12.   *THE TWELFTH STEP TO ONE HUNDRED PER CENT ANSWERED PRAYER IS: PRAY ONLY FOR WHAT YOU SEE THE FATHER DOING.*

Then answered Jesus and said unto them, Verily, verily, I say unto you, The Son can do nothing of himself, but

WHAT HE SEETH THE FATHER DO: for what things soever he doeth, these also doeth the Son likewise.

John 5:19

If you pray about things that cannot be answered, you will only erode your confidence in prayer. If you pray about things that God is not doing, He will not answer you. Jesus avoided praying for something when the Father was not doing it. "And this is the confidence that we have in him, that, if we ask any thing ACCORDING TO HIS WILL, he heareth us" (1 John 5:14).

This is yet another step to gaining one hundred per cent answers to your prayers. God has given us His Spirit to lead us in specific situations. You must be led by the Holy Spirit when you are praying and you must pray for His will. Many pastors are unsuccessful in their prayers because God is not leading them specifically in their prayers.

Once Jesus visited a hospital. There were multitudes of sick people there. However, He prayed for only one person.

After this there was a feast of the Jews; and Jesus went up to Jerusalem. Now there is at Jerusalem by the sheep market a pool, which is called in the Hebrew tongue Bethesda, having five porches.

In these lay a great multitude of impotent folk, of blind, halt, withered, waiting for the moving of the water. For an angel went down at a certain season into the pool, and troubled the water: whosoever then first after the troubling of the water stepped in was made whole of whatsoever disease he had.

And a certain man was there, which had an infirmity thirty and eight years. When Jesus saw him lie, and knew that he had been now a long time in that case, he saith unto him, Wilt thou be made whole? The impotent man answered him, Sir, I have no man, when the water is

troubled, to put me into the pool: but while I am coming, another steppeth down before me. Jesus saith unto him, Rise, take up thy bed, and walk.

John 5:1-8

Why did He not pray for the other hundreds of people who needed help? Jesus operated in these very steps to getting one hundred per cent results. He only dealt with cases He knew would give Him positive results!

It may be God's will to heal everybody. Perhaps the circumstances under which everyone became ill were different. Perhaps in God's plan, it was not yet time for certain healings to manifest.

Jesus knew that it was difficult to get involved in things that God was not doing. Jesus explained why He prayed for only one sick person when there were hundreds who needed a miracle. He said, "I do what I see my Father doing." In other words, if it is not something that God is actively and presently involved in, I will not even bother to pray about it. It may be legally right to do something, but it is very difficult to succeed in something if God is not presently involved with it. If Jesus did not pray difficult prayers, why should you bother?

Then answered Jesus and said unto them, Verily, verily, I say unto you, The Son can do nothing of himself, but WHAT HE SEETH THE FATHER DO: for what things soever he doeth, these also doeth the Son likewise.

John 5:19

If you do not use these principles, you will soon say that God does not answer prayers. Dear friend, it is very possible to get only a "*yes*" answer from God for *all* your requests, if you can diligently practise the steps outlined in this book. Obviously, God will have to say "*no*" when you ask Him for things which are impossible for Him to do.

Take for example Joab, the army commander of King David. Joab killed an innocent man and David cursed him. King David cursed Joab's family forever. He said:

Let it rest on the head of Joab, and on all his father's house; and let there not fail from the house of Joab one that hath an issue, or that is a leper, or that leaneth on a staff, or that falleth on the sword, or that lacketh bread.

2 Samuel 3:29

If you study the details of this curse you will find out that sickness was to be a permanent part of Joab's family. Anyone who found himself praying for Joab's family would find himself praying a difficult prayer. It would be difficult, though not impossible, for the Lord to revoke the curse on Joab's family. This curse is different from God's curse on Adam and Eve, in that it was pronounced by a man. Adam's curse was pronounced by God Himself and obviously carries more weight.

Perhaps some of Joab's relatives were at the hospital that Jesus visited. Perhaps that is why God directed Jesus to pray for only one person. Jesus explained that God had led Him to pray for only one person. Perhaps God was not ready to undo the curse on some people's lives. Perhaps God does not have sufficient reason to undo a legal curse that is on certain people and their families.

...Verily, verily, I say unto you, The Son can do nothing of himself, but what he seeth the Father do...

John 5:19

Allow yourself to be led whenever you are praying. Pray for what you see the Father doing. Be led by the Spirit when you are praying. Don't rush into complex situations blurting out powerless prayers which God will not answer.